Constructing Cultures

TOPICS IN TRANSLATION

Series Editors: Susan Bassnett (*University of Warwick*)
Edwin Gentzler (*University of Massachusetts, Amherst*)

Editor for Translation in the Commercial Environment:
Geoffrey Samuelsson-Brown (*Aardvark Translation Services Ltd*)

Other Books in the Series

Other Books of Interest

Please contact us for the latest book information:
Multilingual Matters, Frankfurt Lodge, Clevedon Hall,
Victoria Road, Clevedon, BS21 7HH, England
http:/www.multi.demon.co.uk

TOPICS IN TRANSLATION 11
Series Editors: Susan Bassnett (*University of Warwick*)
Edwin Gentzler (*University of Massachusetts, Amherst*)

Constructing Cultures
Essays on Literary Translation

Susan Bassnett and André Lefevere

MULTILINGUAL MATTERS
Clevedon • Philadelphia • Toronto • Sydney • Johannesburg

Library of Congress Cataloging in Publication Data

Bassnett, Susan
Constructing Cultures: Essays on Literary Translation/Susan Bassnett and André
Lefevere. Topics in Translation: 11
Includes bibliographical references and index.
1. Translating and interpreting. I. Lefevere, André. II. Title. III. Series.
PN241.B264   1998
418'.02–dc21   97-47653

British Library Cataloguing in Publication Data

A CIP catalogue record for this book is available from the British Library.

ISBN 1-85359-353-2 (hbk)
ISBN 1-85359-352-4 (pbk)

Multilingual Matters Ltd

UK: Frankfurt Lodge, Clevedon Hall, Victoria Road, Clevedon BS21 7HH.
USA: 1900 Frost Road, Suite 101, Bristol, PA 19007, USA.
Canada: OISE, 712 Gordon Baker Road, Toronto, Ontario, Canada M2H 3R7.
Australia: P.O. Box 586, Artamon, NSW, Australia.
South Africa: PO Box 1080, Northcliffe 2115, Johannesburg, South Africa.

Printed and bound in Great Britain by
Marston Book Services Ltd, Oxford

Contents

Preface

SUSAN BASSNETT

The idea for this book emerged from a series of post-graduate seminars that took place at the University of Warwick in the 1990s. André Lefevere was Honorary Professor at Warwick and every year he would come over to England from his home base in Austin, Texas, to talk to students and share views on developments in Translation Studies. Just before his sudden tragic death from leukemia in 1996, he sent me the essays in this volume in draft form. There was no possibility of reciprocation, and though he had heard earlier versions of my essays in lecture form, he never had the opportunity to offer any critical comment on any of them.

Translation is above all a dialogic process, and our working method for years had been dialogic also. This volume should have gone through many more transformations as we read and reread one another's work and rewrote in response to one another's comments. Sadly, the present volume is far too monolingual, though this means that any blame for its shortcomings can be placed firmly on my shoulders alone.

There is a great deal of exciting, innovative thinking going on in Translation Studies at the present time. The subject has come of age, and there are many different approaches, different schools and different perspectives. This is as it should be; all of it is not necessarily congenial to everyone with an interest in the field, but the very fact of diversity is a statement of the successful dissemination of ideas in an interdisciplinary area that has only recently established itself with any seriousness in the academic world.

André Lefevere and I came to work together because of the similarities in our approach to the field. We came into Translation Studies originally for a number of reasons: on a personal level, we had both been educated as bilinguals and were fascinated, as all bilinguals are, with linguistic and cultural difference. Similarly, we had both acquired experience as translators and interpreters and consequently approached theoretical questions from a practical starting point. We were always concerned to make theoretical concepts accessible, since we saw the accessibility of ideas of a means of bridging the gap between those who define themselves as translation scholars and those who define themselves as translators. That such a gap between theorists and practitioners should have existed for so long disadvantages all parties.

Our greatest point of contact, however, lay in the fact that we both saw the study of literary translation(and we have always, unashamedly been interested principally in literary translation) as intimately linked to the study of comparative literature, and we further saw the study of literature as indissolubly connected to history. Quite independently, we came to the conclusion that the relationship between comparative literature and translation studies had worked to the disadvantage of the latter and we sought a change of perspective, arguing that Translation Studies should be seen as the discipline within which comparative literature might be located, rather than the other way round.

The present collection of essays reflects our shared interest in comparative literature and in literary and cultural history. All these essays derive from lectures given to students all over the world, and we are grateful for all the discussions that helped shape our ideas . We are also especially grateful to those colleagues who have helped with the making of this book, in particular Roger Bell, Edwin Gentzler, Piotr Kuhiwczak and Maria Tymoczko.

Foreword

EDWIN GENTZLER

In their work over the past twenty years, Susan Bassnett and André Lefevere have consistently built bridges within the field of translation studies and developed interdisciplinary connections to fields of study outside the discipline. In 1990, they were the first to suggest that translation studies take the 'cultural turn' and look toward work of cultural studies scholars. In their new book *Constructing Cultures*, they present a strong case for moving the field of cultural studies closer to translation studies. New strategies gleaned from translation histories, such as we see in Lefevere's discussion of *Aeneid* translations or Bassnett's discussions of *Inferno* translations that follow, not only give translators more insight into the actual practice of translation, but they also give cultural studies critics new insight into cultural manipulation by those in power. Following Bassnett and Lefevere, translators have increasingly become more empowered and less self-effacing, a development that has allowed theorists to better view the process of mediating between cultures and/or of introducing different words, forms, cultural nuances, and meaning into their own respective culture. As Bassnett and Lefevere argue in *Constructing Cultures*, the study of translation *is* the study of cultural interaction, and thus the appeal of this book to cultural studies scholars, literary theorists, anthropologists, ethnographers, psycholinguists, and language philosophers and all of those interested in multicultural socialisation processes.

Constructing Cultures builds on a series of landmark texts by Bassnett and Lefevere, who, perhaps more than any other scholars in the field, have been responsible for putting translation studies on the academic map. Both were present at the historic 1976 conference in Leuven (Louvain), Belgium, which most scholars agree was the conference at which translation studies was founded. In the collected papers of that conference entitled *Literature and Translation* (Holmes *et al.*, 1978), Lefevere contributed the essay 'Translation: The Focus of the Growth of Literary Knowledge', which traces the linguistic, literary, and cultural components of translation studies, topics that are further elaborated in essays that follow in this anthology. His often quoted 'Translation Studies: The Goal of the Discipline', also collected in the 1978 anthology, argues that translation practice should inform theory and vice versa, a dynamic that has allowed the field to grow so productively. In the same anthology, Bassnett's essay 'Translating Spatial Poetry: An Examination of the Theatre Texts in Performance', expands the purely linguistic and literary methodologies for study to include intertextual and intersemiotic factors, again topics further developed in essays collected here. Bassnett went on to write the book *Translation Studies* (1980), a book that remains the definitive text in the field. Bassnett provides scholars with an historical survey of theoretical developments as well as illuminating samples of comparative analysis. She also discusses strategies for practising translators of poetry, drama, and fiction, again showing how translation theory and comparative analysis can inform practice.

In 1985, the next milestone in the development of the field of translation studies appeared: *The Manipulation of Literature* (1985), edited by Theo Hermans. The title of the anthology ended up giving this group of contributing scholars, including Bassnett and Lefevere, the nickname 'The Manipulation School', a name some associated with the new discipline resisted, but one which in some ways is appropriate. For translation studies scholars were beginning to show that translations, rather than being a secondary and derivative genre, were instead one of the *primary* literary tools that larger social institutions — educational systems, arts councils, publishing firms, and even governments — had at their disposal to 'manipulate' a given society in order to 'construct' the kind of 'culture' desired. Churches would commission Bible translations; governments would support national epic translations; schools would teach great book translations; kings would be patrons for heroic conquests translations; socialist regimes would underwrite socialist realism translations. The 'manipulation' thesis posited in 1985 evolves into 'cultural construction' of the anthology in your hand. The present analysis is much more sophisticated and complex than some of the early ideas, but the ideas posited then have held up to academic and cultural scrutiny.

The *Manipulation of Literature* contained significant contributions by Bassnett and Lefevere. In 'Ways Through the Labyrinth: Strategies and Methods for Translating Theatre Texts', Bassnett suggested including more semiotic markers — gestures, lighting, sound, silences, etc. — than just verbal signs in her methodology for translating drama texts. One can see the development of her thought over the past decade in the essay 'Still Trapped in the Labyrinth' that follows in the present volume. Lefevere contributed the essay 'Why Waste our Time on Rewrites? The Trouble with the Role of Rewriting in an Alternative Paradigm', in which he lays out his concept of 'rewriting' — a genre that includes interpretation, criticism, anthologising, as well as translation — and shows how all rewriters operate under constraints of poetic norms and ideological beliefs inherent in the target culture. We see the development of his pioneering ideas in essays such as 'Translation Practice(s) and the Circulation of Cultural Capital: Some *Aeneids* in English' and 'Acculturating Bertolt Brecht' in the essays that follow in this book.

A real breakthrough for the field of translation studies came in the 1990s with the collection of essays titled *Translation, History, and Culture*, co-edited by Bassnett and Lefevere. It was then that translation studies officially took the 'cultural turn', the authors redefining the object of study as a verbal text within the network of literary and extra-literary signs in both the source and target cultures. As Bassnett notes in Chapter 8, 'The Translation Turn in Cultural Studies', that follows, she and Lefevere were suggesting that such a redefinition of the field

> could offer a way of understanding how complex manipulative textual processes take place: how a text is selected for translation ... what role the translator plays in that selection, what the role of an editor, publisher, or patron plays, what criteria determine the strategies that will be employed for the translators, and how a text might be received in the target system.

While many scholars were inching toward the cultural turn in the early 1990s, Bassnett and Lefevere were the first to articulate the position. In the explosion of events that have followed, Bassnett and Lefevere again have led the way.

In 1992, Lefevere published not just one, but *three* books on translation: *Translation, Rewriting, and the Manipulation of Literary Fame, Translation/ History/Culture: A Sourcebook*, and *Translating Literature*. In addition, he published them not with obscure firms, but with major publishing firms such as Routledge and MLA Press. The books sold well, and the boom in translation studies was on. New journals such as *The Translator* and *Target* sprang up. Conference activity increased all over the world, including England, Holland, Poland, Finland, Spain, Austria, Brazil, and Canada. New publishing firms got into the market, e.g., Kent State University Press in the USA or Jerome Publishing in England. Old series were revived, such as the Rodopi Series in Holland. Encyclopedias of translation studies were developed in England, Germany, China, and elsewhere. Perhaps most significantly, translation studies entered academia, with new MA and PhD programmes starting at universities such as Middlesex, Massachusetts, Salamanca, São Paulo, and elsewhere. It is a shame that André Lefevere is no longer with us and is unable to see the fruits of the seeds that he planted.

In many ways, *Constructing Cultures* can be viewed as a celebration of André Lefevere's life and work. Everyone in the field, most deeply Susan Bassnett, perhaps his closest colleague and friend, is saddened by his passing. With difficulty and great care, Bassnett has collected and edited his final words in the shape that follows here.

The explosion of thinking and writing on and about translations has made it hard for anyone to keep up. For those recently discovering the field, Bassnett's and Lefevere's *Constructing Cultures* offer a variety of essays that reflect the evolution of the field: these essays address the most recent developments in theory, in cultural studies, in translation research (called descriptive studies by translation studies scholars), and in teaching translation. Susan Bassnett and André Lefevere also continue to push the boundaries of the definition of the field of translation studies. This book is not just a collection of essays and talks presented at colloquia of the past and/or previously published in journals. Rather, it presents new and unpublished material, either in the form of new work the two of them had presented in process at closed seminars of the graduate programme at the Centre for British and Comparative Cultural Studies at the University of Warwick, or radically rethinking and revising positions taken in previously published essays.

Constructing Cultures begins with three new essays: first, the introduction co-authored by Bassnett and Lefevere entitled 'Where are we in Translation Studies?'; then the first chapter by Lefevere entitled 'Chinese and Western Thinking on Translation'; and next the second chapter by Bassnett entitled 'When is Translation not a Translation?'. The co-authored introductory essay combines a blend of translation history followed by a new set of questions and openings for future research. It also contains the central thesis of the book, and answers a question those who first pick up the book might ask. Why is a book by two prominent translation scholars called *Constructing Cultures*? The answer indicates just how far translation studies has evolved since 1978. Translators, argue Bassnett and Lefevere, have always provided a vital link enabling different cultures to interact. The next logical stage posited by Bassnett and Lefevere is not just to study translations but to study cultural interaction. Perhaps the most obvious, comprehensive, indeed empirical data for studying cultural interaction are the translated texts themselves. To do so, Bassnett and Lefevere posit three models for studying translations that they have found useful: the Horatian model, in which the translator tends to be faithful to his/her customers, i.e., the target audience; the Jerome model, in which the translator tends to be faithful to the source text, in this case the Bible; and the Schleiermacher model, which emphasises preservation of the alterity of the source model for the target reader. Rather than suggesting that one theory of translation is valid across cultures and time, Bassnett's and Lefevere's multiple models are helpful for studying translations in different cultures during different periods. They also offer new critical tools to enable such study, such as the concept of 'textual grids' derived from the work of Pierre Bourdieu. A textual grid is understood as the collection of acceptable literary forms and genres in which texts can be expressed. For example, Chinese novels have their own set of rules, rules which differ from the ways in which novels in Europe tend to be constructed. These 'grids' cause patterns of expectations in the respective audiences, and both practising translators and in particular literary historians need to take into consideration such grids in order to better produce and/or analyse translations. Of most interest in the introductory essay are the set of questions Bassnett and Lefevere ask. For example, why are certain texts translated and not others? What is the agenda behind translation? How are translators used by those in control of such agendas? Can we predict how a given translation might function in any given culture? The future of the field is bright, according to Bassnett and Lefevere; areas for future research include, among others, the study of the history of translation to better relativise the present, the study of postcolonial translation to better re-evaluate Eurocentric models, and the study of different kinds of criticism, anthologies, reference works, as well as translations, to see how images of texts are created and function within any given culture.

In Chapter 1, 'Chinese and Western Thinking on Translation', André Lefevere shows how a textual grid might help scholars doing comparative analysis. He views the concept of translation historically, showing just how culturally dependent our Western definition is. In a fascinating essay that juxtaposes the history of translation in the West and China, we see that our definition (white, Anglo-Germanic) of translation may not be as universal as some theorists speculate. Lefevere compares a system in the West in which translations are invariably written by a single author and read in silence by single readers to a system in China in which translations tend to be oral in nature, often translated by teams of scholars, and frequently recited and/or chanted publicly. In the West, he suggests, the 'original' text always consciously or subconsciously looms behind the translated text, whereas in China, the translated text often *replaces* the original, with the reader asking few questions about the 'original'. Lefevere examines powerful institutions that may shape such sensibilities such as the Roman Catholic Church in the West and powerful emperors in China. As a result, Lefevere forces the reader to see that our very definition of translation as a kind of language transfer is embedded in larger systems or grids that define and limit our practice to a greater degree than hitherto imagined. Only by taking a step back from the immediate language transfer process, and by taking the larger institutions involved in cultural construction into consideration can the scholar begin to see the nature of the role translations play in cultural construction.

Lefevere continues to explore the usefulness of the concept of a textual grid throughout the book that follows. For example, in Chapter 5, 'The Gates of Analogy: The *Kalevala* in English', Lefevere examines the construction and translations of the Kalevala, a collection of Finnish oral poetry, a kind of Finnish national epic, to show how readers and critics consciously and unconsciously submit to a culturally constructed concept of an acceptable form for national epics, a 'grid' influenced by our concept of Homeric epics or Nordic epics. Lefevere argues that submitting to such a grid that underlies our notion of 'world literature' is particularly important to literatures written in languages less widely spoken. If a nation wants to recognised as a nation among world nations, as was true of Finland in the late eighteenth and early nineteenth century, then constructing a national epic is one of the main requirements. Lefevere shows that that very construction was exactly what a series of Finnish critics and translators set out to do. Quoting *Kalevala* translator Keith Bosley, Lefevere points out that the Finnish historians who constructed the epic were 'concerned less with fidelity to sources than with the validation of a national culture'. Ironically, because of the predominance of the Swedish language in Finland at the time, the very scholars who constructed the Finnish epic had to do so using *Swedish* at first, the only literary language they knew. For lesser-known languages such as Finnish, Czech, Flemish, Gaelic, such a ironic twist is not unusual; their revival is often dependent upon translations from Swedish, German, French, or English to bring them into existence. In 'The *Kalevala* in English', Lefevere shows that both critics such as Lönnrot and translators such as the first two English translators very definitely use grids such as those of the classical Nordic epic to manipulate the original to conform to what readers typically associate with classical epics. This kind of research on the role translations play in emerging nations is one of the most exciting contributions of translation studies scholars. Pioneering work by translation studies scholars such as Lefevere provide us with models from the past that will have enormous influence on cultural studies and identity formation in the future.

One of the most fascinating texts illustrating the phenomenon of the construction of a national epic via translation is James Macpherson's translation of *Ossian*, a Scottish national epic, right around the same time Finnish scholars were constructing the *Kalevala*. The only problem was that

no original existed. Macpherson's translation was a hoax, or what translation studies has come to call a 'pseudo-translation', a term coined by Gideon
Toury in 'Translation, Literary Translation, and Pseudotranslation' (1985).
Lefevere's essay on the translation of 'epic' literature in lesser-known
languages is complemented by Susan Bassnett's essay in Chapter 2, 'When
is a Translation Not a Translation?' She, too, points out how cultural
construction is a determinant factor in presenting and marketing a text as
a translation, when it is in fact an original work. Why might someone do
such a thing? Often certain cultural constraints make it impossible to write
about certain topics or use certain poetic forms. In the USA, for example,
with free verse reigning as the norm in poetic circles, publishing serious
verse in rhymed couplets might be difficult; however, if one masked one's
identity and posed as the greatest writer from some other country, perhaps
one could perhaps find one's way into print. Examples of such deception
abound, including the recent publication of the work of 'Araki Yasusada'
in English. Yasusada, a Japanese Hiroshima 'survivor', writes poems whose
surreal images and abrupt juxtapositions were in stark contrast to the often
sentimental images of other Hiroshima poets translated into English. The
problem was Yasusada didn't exist. While rumours are still flying, the lead
suspect, according to Emily Nussbaum (1997) in 'Turning Japanese; The
Hiroshima Poetry Hoax' is one Kent Johnson, professor of English and
Spanish at Highland Community College, who has published his own
poems in the voice of a Hiroshima survivor, masking his identity to lend
authenticity to his voice. The difference between an imagined survivor and
a 'real' Japanese survivor/eyewitness are two different things, especially
when one considers that the constructed biography of Yasusada includes
his daughter dying of radiation poisoning.

   In 'When is Translation Not a Translation?' Bassnett introduces a new
concept she calls 'collusion' to analyse such pseudo-translations, arguing
that readers go along with this ruse for a variety of conscious and
subconscious reasons. Given the number of examples she cites, pseudo-
translations are much more prevalent than the reading public and/or
literary critics ever imagined: Thomas Mallory's *Morte d'Arthur*, Richard
Burton's *The Kasidah of Hají Abdú El-Yezdí* are pseudo-translations; others
are found within travel writing texts such as Robert Byron's *The Road to
Oxiana*, in which dialogues are presented as translations, but the reader
subconsciously knows that the traveller does *not* know the indigenous
language; thus they must indeed be fabricated rather than factual. Because
readers do not want to admit this, readers 'collude' with the writer in
perpetuating the facade that these texts and/or dialogues are based on 'fact'
rather than fiction. The scheme also allows the original writer to remain the

authority and effectively erases the translator from the mediatory process. Bassnett's insights point out just how difficult it is to determine the border between original writing and translation and how critics 'collude' with a culture that tends to have very distinct and separate concepts of original writing and translation. Such thinking makes *Constructing Culture* appeal to cultural studies scholars and language philosophers alike.

Bassnett and Lefevere deploy these new critical tools well in *Constructing Cultures* when they revisit sites of their thinking about translation developed during their earlier years. In Chapter 3, 'Translation Practice(s) and the Circulation of Cultural Capital: Some *Aeneids* in English', Lefevere provides a diachronic study of translations of the *Aeneid* into English, the kind of translation history characteristic of translation studies during its descriptive phase of the 1980s. This time, however, Lefevere incorporates the concept of 'cultural capital' from Pierre Bourdieu, by which he refers to information a person needs in any given cultural context to belong to the 'right circles', information that Lefevere argues is regulated and transmitted by translation. Attacking translation critics who set up some sort of universal standard of good versus bad to judge translations and to explain their success or failure in a given culture, Lefevere instead argues that the success of certain translation of Virgil's *Aeneid* has to do less with the quality of the translation, and more to do with the *prestige* of the source language culture for the audience of the translation, i.e., the elite reading public (whose skill in Latin is decreasing over time) in England who want to belong to the right literary and social circles. Behind this article we see the concept of patronage developed by Lefevere. For example, in a 1984 essay called 'That Structure in the Dialect of Man Interpreted', Lefevere talked about patronage as any kind of force that can be influential in encouraging or discouraging, even censoring, works of literature. Lefevere's concept of patronage is a broad one: kings, queens, booksellers, school systems, arts councils, governments, are all implicated. In the case of 'Some *Aeneids* in English', Lefevere gives the example of the Pope serving as a patron for Christopher Pitt's 1740 translation, or the broadcasting industry serving as a patron in the case of Cecil Day Lewis' 1952 translation. What I find interesting in this essay is that Lefevere actually uses his theory to predict future translations, arguing for example that patrons of feminist bookstores will no doubt contribute to the production of a new feminist translation of the *Aeneid*.

On goal of Lefevere's work is to unmask institutional forces that create a kind of translation hegemony which influences the kinds of translation that get produced. In Chapter 7, 'Acculturating Bertolt Brecht', Lefevere turns to the literary criticism industry and uses the example of Brecht translations in the USA to illustrate his point. Although he dealt with Brecht translations previously in his essay 'Mother Courage's Cucumbers' (1982), this time he expands the parameters of translation studies to include both translations, literary criticism, and reference works such as encyclopedias. Using his concept of translation as a kind of 'rewriting', introduced in 1987 in an article called '"Beyond Interpretation" or the Business of (Re)Writing', and referring to all those writers who interpret, explain, paraphrase literary texts. Lefevere reveals how both translators and literary critics are guilty of perpetuating certain cultural values at the expense of others as they rewrite. This new essay 'Acculturating Bertolt Brecht' exposes literary and ideological prejudices in the United States during the World War II period through the early 1970s, and demonstrates how translators and critics were not innocent bystanders of such cultural prejudices, but rather active participants contributing to particular cultural constructions. Discussing *Mother Courage* translations by H.R. Hays (1941), Eric Bentley (1967), and Ralph Manheim (1972), for example, Lefevere reveals the leading role translators played in making Brecht part of the American canon. While the translators' negotiations to make Brecht accepted tended to remain at the level of language, stage directions, and literary form, Lefevere goes on to argue that the real critical battle over the reception of Brecht was waged by the literary critics. In his analysis of the criticism, Lefevere shows another kind of collusion, in which critics ignored Brecht's epic forms and alienation effects, dismissed his politics and Marxism, and instead turned Brecht into another kind of liberal humanist. Lefevere's quotes are especially damning: Bentley, for example, sublates 'epic theatre' into 'theatre of narrative realism'; Brocket turns Brecht's alienation effects into another kind of Aristotelian catharsis. Some critics went so far as to argue that Brecht's Marxism damaged his work and that Brecht's primary significance was his ability to 'entertain'. The powerful combination of critics and translators succeeded in constructing an *image* of Brecht in the West for those who do not know German. For those who do, such a social constructing is actually appalling; one begins to wonder whether there are any professional standards in literary translation or literary criticism at all. One of the goals of translation studies over the past two decades has been to reveal the social and literary norms of the target culture and show the impact that such constraints have on practising translators; Lefevere's essay not only effectively demonstrates such constraints, but it also shows how translators and critics participate in that very construction. For those postcolonial critics who are attempting to unmask cultural institutions that serve to marginalise minority voices and for those with alternative political persuasions, one can learn much from

Lefevere's essay. Such translation studies research might also inform the training of literary and cultural critics as well.

Armed with a new set of critical tools, Bassnett also productively revisits a site of her previous thinking, i.e., that of theatre translation, in Chapter 6, 'Still Trapped in the Labyrinth: Further Reflections on Translation and Theatre'. Less than comfortable with certain literary critical notions prevalent in the West, Bassnett uses examples of third world translations to illustrate her points. Playing with the overlapping boundaries among play text, translation, and performance, she expands the boundaries of translation studies to include visual as well as verbal signs. The central argument circles around Bassnett's discomfort with certain scholars' notion of 'performability', i.e., those who claim that a kind of universal 'performability' (or 'speakablity' or 'gestic subtext') is inherit in the text, one that determines whether or not the play can be translated and/or performed in the first place. Indeed, Bassnett sees a danger in such universalising concepts: for once the translator/director has a vision of this elusive universal gestic subtext, many contradictions, subtle nuances, and shifts in tone in the text may get smoothed out for the sake of a unified conceptual vision. Using well chosen examples, such as Vicki Ooi's discussion of the translation of O'Neill's *Long Day's Journey into Night* into Chinese, Bassnett shows how certain non-Western cultures do not have the convention of searching for subtextual patterns within a playtext. One of the strengths of both Bassnett and Lefevere's work over the years has been the fact that they are not interested in theory as philosophy, but in theory that may be of use for *practising* translators. Indeed, very little practical advice exists for those translating drama. Yet here Bassnett offers explicit and well-taken advice: trying to render a text performable is *not* the translator's task; rather, Bassnett recommends leaving in the contradictions, nuances, and shifts in tone if found in the original. The director, the dramaturge, or the actor, may end up unifying the text. The goal of the translator, however, is *to maintain the strangeness* of the text in order to allow the reader (or artistic director) to discover the text for themselves. In fact, the only way to construct a multicultural theatre in the West will be if translators reject strategies that conform to Western dramatic conventions and cultural practices, reject searching for deep, unifying structures, and instead focus on the translation of the signs of the texts — the words, the silences, the shifts of tone — in all their the contradictions and multi-layered play.

Bassnett further blends theory and practical advice in Chapter 4, 'Transplanting the Seed: Poetry and Translation'. Her advice for poetry translators is similar to the advice she gives theatre translators: to focus on the play of language in the text. Bassnett distances herself from notions that poetry is some intangible, ineffable spirit or presence, taking issue with poets such as Robert Frost who suggest that poetry is what gets lost in translation. Supporting a thesis posited by poet and translator Frederic Will (1993) in *Translation, Theory and Practice: Reassembling the Tower*, Bassnett argues that texts consist of language — nouns, verbs, grammatical patterns — the very material with which translators work with to construct their translations. Citing famous translators such as Ezra Pound, Augusto de Campos, Yves Bonnefoy, and Octavio Paz, Bassnett argues the task of the translator is to dismantle the raw linguistic material of the poet, and to reassemble the signs in a new language. The task is less to copy an original, but to compose an analogous text. Paz suggests we think in terms of transmutation; Bassnett suggests that we think in terms of transplanting a seed. To illustrate her theory, Bassnett gives several illuminating examples of both how to and how not to translate. She cites, for example, Sir Thomas Wyatt's translations of Petrarch as an example of Paz' translation approach. While some critics are uncomfortable with Wyatt's translation strategy, Bassnett is not. She allows that Wyatt makes many changes, including altering the rhyme scheme and foregrounding many pronouns, especially the self-referential 'I', which makes the poetry less mystical and more concrete. Yet by subtly altering the form, Bassnett shows how Wyatt created a new form with new possibilities in the English language, one that was later to be used by writers such as Sidney, Spenser, and Shakespeare. The seed, once transplanted, flourishes. She also gives excellent examples of how not to translate, citing several versions of the Paolo and Francesca story from Dante's *Inferno*, Canto V. In a typical translation studies fashion, Bassnett compares translations by Cary (1816), Byron (1820), Longfellow (1867), Norton (1941), Sayers (1949), Sisson (1980) and Durling (1996). What strikes the reader is how confusing and devoid of feeling nearly all of them are. The signs never become free, but instead remain tied to their source, clumsily bound to two syntactic structures, and uncertain with regard to their intended audience. Bassnett hopes to liberate translators from their slavish attachment to the source text, and empower them with positive imagery. Bassnett views translation as energy-releasing, as freeing linguistic and semiotic signs to circulate among the best creative writing in the receiving culture. Such a theory of translation has post-structuralist resonance; one can hear echoes of Benjamin, Derrida, and de Man in Bassnett's position; recent work of translation studies scholars such as Lawrence Venuti and Teraswini Niranjani indicate its growing acceptance in the field. Yet, perhaps most importantly, is the appeal of such a translation approach for cultural studies and postcolonial scholars.

Susan Bassnett's final essay 'The Translation Turn in Cultural Studies' makes the connection between translation studies and cultural studies. A fitting conclusion to this book, the essay announces a new era for interdisciplinary research. Translation studies scholarship over the last three decades has now built up what might be called a critical mass of scholarship, enough that any cultural studies scholars discussing intercultural movement, or lamenting the lack thereof, needs to consult the findings of the translation studies scholarship. I have argued that translated texts serve as empirical data documenting intercultural transfer; Bassnett argues similarly that translations are the *performative* aspect of intercultural communication. Using models developed by Anthony Easthope in a recent essay 'But what *is* Cultural Studies' (1997), Bassnett traces a parallel development of both cultural studies and translation studies over the past three decades, both going through a culturalist phase (Nida and Newmark), a structuralist phase (Even-Zohar and Toury), and a post-structuralist phase (Simon and Niranjana). As cultural studies now enters a new internationalist phase, incorporating sociological and ethnographic methodologies, Bassnett suggests that the moment has come for the two disciplines to jump off their parallel track and join together. Cultural studies is now dealing with questions of power relations and textual production. Translation studies scholars know something about this: their years of research in historical comparison of Greek and Latin classics or canonical writers such as Dante, Shakespeare, Goethe, have given them great insight into how cultural values and ideals are constructed and whose interests such values represent. Yet while cultural studies has embraced gender studies, film studies, and media studies, Bassnett points out that they have been slow to recognise the value of translation studies research. Quoting Homi Bhabha's citation of Paul de Man from *The Location of Culture* (1994), Bassnett argues that translations provide the scholar with actual situations of cultural transfer rather than hypothetical situations: translation, de Man notes, 'puts the original in motion to decanonise it, giving it movement of fragmentation, a wandering of errance, a kind of permanent exile'. For Bassnett, this image of translation as a sign of fragmentation, wandering, and exile, characterises the new internationalist phase of cultural studies in the late twentieth century. More than a metaphor, Bassnett concludes, the study of culture would do well to study the processes of encoding and decoding involved in translation. For in the study of translations, the scholar can demonstrate how fragments survive, which wanderings occur, and how texts in exile are received. As Barbara Johnson (1985) has argued in 'Taking Fidelity Philosophically', a text that Bassnett has cited in the past, it is time to move the study of translations from the margins of critical investigations to centre stage. Translation studies has taken the cultural turn; now cultural studies should take the translation turn.

In *Constructing Cultures*, Bassnett and Lefevere again present the field with a pioneering text. For the past two decades, translation studies has conducted much descriptive work. The methodology has been sound, the comparisons valid, and the values and interests of the cultural elite in various European and North American societies exposed. Yet much of this work has been carried out behind the scenes and has not yet reached wider audiences. Many scholars in the field have been asking where will translation studies go after its descriptive studies period. In *Constructing Cultures*, Bassnett and Lefevere not only report on the latest developments in the field of translation studies, they also point to new directions for the discipline for the next millennium. When I read work by Jacques Derrida, Homi Bhabha, or Edward Said, I am often struck by how naive their ideas about translation sound in comparison to the detailed analysis provided by translation scholars. Bassnett and Lefevere point the field to a new interdisciplinary phase. As cultural studies scholars, postcolonial critics, and language philosophers discover translation studies, they should like what they see. Translation studies scholars need also to learn from methods of cultural studies disciplines to broaden their investigations. In 'The Translation Turn', Bassnett points to new avenues for interdisciplinary investigations into what Venuti calls the 'ethnocentric violence of translation', into how cultures construct 'images' of writers, and into which texts become cultural capital for the ruling elite. The task is large, for no one scholar from any single discipline can fully comprehend the complex network of signs that constitute a culture. Bassnett forcefully argues that we need to combine resources, broaden research, and begin a new era of intercultural training, thereby opening the field to a plurality of voices.

References

Bassnett, Susan (1980) *Translation Studies*. London: Methuen. (Rev. edition: London: Routledge, 1988).

Bassnett, Susan and André Lefevere (eds) (1990) *Translation, History, and Culture*. London: Pinter.

Bhabha, Homi (1994) *The Location of Culture*. London: Routledge.

Easthope, Anthony (1997) But what *is* Cultural Studies. In Susan Bassnett (ed.) *Studying British Cultures: An Introduction*. London: Routledge.

Hermans, Theo (1985) *The Manipulation of Literature*. New York: St. Martins Press.

Holmes, James S., Lambert, José and van den Broek, Raymond (eds) (1978) *Literature and Translation: New Perspectives in Literary Studies*. Leuven: Acco.

Johnson, Barbara (1985) Taking fidelity philosophically. In Joseph F. Graham (ed.) *Difference in Translation*. Ithaca: Cornell University Press.

Lefevere, André (1982) Mother Courage's Cucumbers: Text, system, and refraction in a theory of literature. *Modern Language Studies* 12 (4) (Fall), 3–20.

Lefevere, André (1992a) *Translation, Rewriting, and the Manipulation of Literary Fame*. London: Routledge.

Lefevere, André (1992b) *Translation/History/Culture: A Sourcebook*. London: Routledge.

Lefevere, André (1992c) *Translating Literature*. New York: MLA Press.

Nussbaum, Emily (1997) Turning Japanese: The Hiroshima poetry hoax. *Lingua Franca* 6 (7) (November), 82–84.

Toury, Gideon (1985) Translation, literary translation, and pseudotranslation. *Comparative Criticism* Vol. 6. Cambridge: Cambridge University Press.

Will, Frederic (1993) *Translation, Theory and Practice: Reassembling the Tower*. Lampeter: Edwin Mellon Press.

Introduction

Where are we in Translation Studies?

ANDRÉ LEFEVERE and SUSAN BASSNETT

Translation Studies Today

The questions that are generally accepted as relevant and important enough to be asked in the field of translation studies are very different now from what they were twenty years ago, when we first began to publish on translation. That fact is perhaps the clearest indicator of the distance we have covered in the meantime. Another indicator is that 'translation studies' has now come to mean something like 'anything that (claims) to have anything to do with translation'. Twenty years ago it meant: training translators. It is amazing to see, with hindsight, how preposterous some of the questions that were asked twenty years ago seem to us now.

The most preposterous question was that of translatability or: 'is translation possible'. The question seems preposterous now because we have discovered the history of translation in the meantime, and that discovery enabled us to counter that question with another, namely: 'why are you interested in proving or disproving the feasibility of something that has been going on around most of the world for at least four thousand years?'

History, then, is one of the things that happened to translation studies since the 1970s, and with history a sense of greater relativity and of the greater importance of concrete negotiations at certain times and in certain places, as opposed to abstract, general rules that would always be valid. In the post-war period, the agenda behind the analysis of translatability was that of the possible development of machines that would make translations valid for all times and all places, and would do so at any time, in any place. Machines, and machines alone, were to be trusted to produce 'good' translations, always and everywhere. History has turned out to be the ghost in that machine, and as the ghost has grown, the machine has crumbled.

Perhaps the most arresting example of this crumbling of the machine is the long retreat, and final disintegration of the once key concept of equivalence. Twenty years ago those in the field would ask themselves whether equivalence, too, was possible, and whether there was a foolproof

1

way to find it if it were possible. Again, the underlying assumption seemed to be that there could be something like an abstract and universally valid equivalence. Today we know that specific translators decide on the specific degree of equivalence they can realistically aim for in a specific text, and that they decide on that specific degree of equivalence on the basis of considerations that have little to do with the concept as it was used two decades ago.

The Jerome Model

The concept of equivalence lies at the heart of what may be called the 'Jerome' model of translation, after Saint Jerome (c.331–c.420 AD) whose Vulgate set the acknowledged and unacknowledged standards of much of translation in the West until about two hundred years ago. In its simplest avatar it reads more or less as follows: there is a text, and that text just needs to be transposed into another language, as faithfully as possible. Faithfulness is insured by good dictionaries, and since anybody can, basically, use a good dictionary, there is really no reason to train translators well, and even less of a reason to pay them well.

The days of the Jerome model are now numbered, at least in the West. The model is characterised by the presence of a central, sacred text, that of the Bible, which must be translated with the utmost fidelity, and the early ideal of that fidelity was the interlinear translation, in which one word would match another, indeed, in which the translated word would be written under the word it was supposed to translate. Even if the interlinear ideal could not be maintained in practice, short of producing a text syntactically so skewed as to become unintelligible, it did remain the ideal, not just for Biblical translation, but also, by extension, for translations of other texts. Precisely because it could never be realised, the ideal continued to haunt translators and those who thought about translation over the centuries. Since it could not be realised, de facto compromises were necessary, which were, of course, entered into, although at the double price of interminable wrangling about precisely how 'faithful' faithfulness should be, or what could really be termed an 'equivalent' of what and, more importantly, of generating a perennial feeling of guilt in translators and of permanently marginalising them in society as necessary evils, more evil at some times, more necessary at others.

To be able to elevate faithfulness to this central position, to the exclusion of many other factors, the Jerome model had to reduce thinking about translation to the linguistic level only. This could be done all the more easily because the text that served as the yardstick for fidelity was seen as timeless and unchangeable precisely because of its sacred nature.

It is because the Bible no longer exerts such powerful influence as a sacred text in the West to the extent it once did, that thinking about translation has been able to move away from the increasingly sterile 'faithful/free' opposition, and that it has been able to redefine equivalence, which is no longer seen as the mechanical matching of words in dictionaries, but rather as a strategic choice made by translators. What has changed is that one type of faithfulness (the one commonly connected with equivalence) is no longer imposed on translators. Rather, they are free to opt for the kind of faithfulness that will ensure, in their opinion, that a given text is received by the target audience in optimal conditions.

The change that has occurred, then, is from the belief in one type of faithfulness, conveniently equated with 'faithfulness as such', to the realisation that there are different types of faithfulness that may be adequate in different situations. After this change, people in the field gradually stopped asking the old questions and started replacing them with the questions that are dominating the field right now. These questions include : 'What is the function of the (this, not a, any) translation likely to be?' 'What type of text needs to be translated?' 'Who is the initiator of the/this translation?' Translations, we have learned, are not faithful or free as such, not 'good' or 'bad' for ever, in all circumstances; rather, it is perfectly possible that they have to be faithful in some situations and free in others, in order to work to the satisfaction of their initiators.

We have learned to ask these questions, and we have realised their relevance, because we are no longer 'stuck to the word', or even the text, because we have realised the importance of context in matters of translation. One context is, of course, that of history. The other context is that of culture. The questions that now dominate the field are able to dominate it because research has taken a 'cultural turn', because people in the field began to realise, some time ago, that translations are never produced in a vacuum, and that they are also never received in a vacuum.

The Horace Model

We are in the process of moving beyond the Jerome model, towards a model that is associated with the name of the Roman poet Horace (65 BC–8 BC) and which historically predates the Jerome model, but has been overshadowed by it for about fourteen centuries. Horace's often quoted, though not always understood, 'fidus interpres' was not faithful to a text, but to *his* customers, and they were his customers only in Horace's time. A 'fidus' translator/interpreter was one who could be trusted, who got the job done on time and to the satisfaction of both parties. To do so, he had to negotiate between two clients and two languages, if he was an interpreter, or between a patron and two languages if he was a translator. The fact that negotiation is the central concept here militates heavily against the kind of faithfulness traditionally associated with equivalence. Indeed, it is entirely conceivable, not to say inevitable, that the interpreter who wants to negotiate successfully a business transaction may, at times, be very well advised not to translate 'faithfully', so as not to let the negotiations collapse. In the Horatian model there is no sacred text, but there definitely is a privileged language, namely Latin. This implies that negotiation is, in the end, always slanted toward the privileged language, and that the negotiation does not take place on absolutely equal terms. The parallels between the position of Latin in Horace's time and English today are interestingly close. English today occupies the same position throughout the world that Latin occupied in the Mediterranean during the last centuries of the republic and the first centuries of the principate. Translations into English, particularly from third world languages, are almost invariably slanted toward English: we are confronted with what we may term the 'Holiday Inn Syndrome', where everything foreign and exotic is standardised, to a great extent. At least this is the case with texts that can be considered to build the 'cultural capital' of a civilisation. The question does not even arise for another type of text, and for reasons that have little to do with translation as such: the day when computer manuals will be translated from Uzbek into English, rather than the other way around, is obviously not near.

Another change is that today, we have come to recognise that different types of texts require different translation strategies. Some texts are primarily designed to convey information, and it stands to reason that translations of such texts should try to convey that information as well as possible. How they do so in practice will, in each particular case, be the result of assumed or explicit negotiation among the initiators who not only want the text translated, but also want it to function in the receiving culture in a meaningful way, the translator who actually translates it, the culture to which the text belongs, the culture the translation is aimed at, and the function the text is supposed to fulfil in the culture the translation is aimed at.

There are also texts that are primarily designed to entertain. They will have to be translated in a different, though not necessarily a radically different manner, since texts that are primarily designed to convey information, may well also try to entertain their readers, if only to ensure that the information will be conveyed in the most painless manner possible. Conversely, texts that are primarily designed to entertain, may, and often do, also contain information.

A third type of texts, which obviously has elements of the other two in them, as well as elements of the fourth type, tries to persuade. The fourth type consists of those texts that are recognised as belonging to the 'cultural capital' of a given culture, or even to the 'cultural capital' of something like 'world culture'. The novels of Trollope would be more 'British' than 'world' cultural capital, the plays of Shakespeare would be both. Texts that are recognised as cultural capital will, obviously, have started out as belonging to one, two, or all three of the other types, and they will continue to influence the other types.

But perhaps more important than the several and separate types is the existence of what can be called a 'grid' of text, the textual grid that a culture makes use of, the collection of acceptable ways in which things can be said. Different cultures may, of course, make use of essentially the same textual grid. The French, German, and English cultures, for instance, make use of the same textual grid, with slight variations in emphasis, because that is the grid they inherited from Greco-Roman antiquity through the shared vicissitudes of history. Other cultures, like Chinese and Japanese culture, have textual grids that are much more unique and not shared with other cultures. The interesting point in all this, though, is that these 'textual grids' seem to exist in cultures on a level that is deeper, or higher, or whatever metaphor you prefer, than that of language. In other words, the 'textual grid' pre-exists language(s). These grids are man-made, historical, contingent constructs; they are by no means eternal, unchangeable, or even 'always already there'. They can, and do, appear given for all eternity only when, as so often happens, they have been interiorised by human beings to such an extent that they have become totally transparent for them, that they appear 'natural'.

If textual grids do exist, and we claim that they do, not explicitly, but as a pattern of expectations that is felt, has been interiorised by members of a culture, who may not be able to list most, or all of their characteristic features and the rules that regulate their production, then students of translation should pay more attention to them than they have in the past, whether they want to learn the technique of translating, or whether they want to analyse translations and the part they play in the evolution of cultures.

One of the great strides that has been made over the last twenty years is the realisation that the house of translation has, indeed, many mansions now, not least because the definition of the field has been widened to include more than just the technique of translating, as it is studied and taught. Yet it would seem that the set of questions identified above as dominating the field, is as valid for the house as a whole as it is for its many mansions. This central set of questions guarantees the unity of the field at its core; beyond that, there is much work, and of various different kinds, to be done in the various subfields, or 'interfields', of translation. It is easy to imagine translation as an interfield of linguistics, for instance, of literature, and of anthropology, cultural and otherwise. Again, while the different interfields can be 'felt' to exist by those working in the larger field, it would not be altogether wise to try to erect barriers between them, since one can, and should, indeed learn from the other whenever necessary.

A tremendous change, perhaps the most tremendous change in the field of translation occurred not when more and more interfields were added, but when the finality, the goal of work in the field was drastically widened. In the 1970s, translation was seen, as it undoubtedly is, as 'vital to the interaction between cultures'. What we have done is to take this statement and stand it on its head: if translation is, indeed, as everybody believes, vital to the interaction between cultures, then why not take the next step and study translation, not just to train translators, but precisely to study cultural interaction? There are no doubt various other ways in which that process can also be studied, but we contend that translation offers a means of studying cultural interaction that is not offered in the same way by any other field. Translation provides researchers with one of the most obvious, comprehensive, and easy to study 'laboratory situations' for the study of cultural interaction. A comparison of original and translation will not only reveal the constraints under which translators have to work at a certain time and in a certain place, but also the strategies they develop to overcome, or at least work around those constraints. This kind of comparison can, therefore, give the researcher something like a synchronic snapshot of many features of a given culture at a given time. Moreover, it can easily be shown that certain translations, and not just of the Bible in the West or the Buddhist Scriptures in China, have exerted an enormous influence on the evolution of societies and, through them, the evolution of history.

Translation is in history, always. It is, in many cases, a vital factor within history, and the more we learn about its history, the more obvious this fact becomes. It is no coincidence, therefore, that many histories of translation have been published over the last ten years, just as it is no exaggeration to say that if we want to study cultural history, the history of philosophy, literature, and religion, we shall have to study translations to a much greater extent than we have done in the past.

If you are a researcher in the field of translation and you think that translation does, and should, promote international understanding, you will define meaningful research in your interfield (which you should not equate with the field as a whole) as the activity that provides those working in that interfield with the tools needed to do their work better, to improve the techniques of translating. If, on the other hand, you think that translation should primarily be used as a tool to analyse the processes through which international understanding comes into being, you will define meaningful research in your interfield (which you should also not equate with the field as a whole) in a different way. In the first case you will produce books and articles aimed at improving the training of translators, you will concern yourself more with translating than with translation. In the second case, you will produce the kind of case studies that are brought together in this book, as possible instances of the direction in which this kind of research could develop. There is no reason why both mansions should not be able to coexist in the house of translation.

The Schleiermacher Model

The case studies collected in this book deal with texts that constitute cultural capital, which should not be equated with capital as it is used in economics, but which makes it easier for people within a culture to gain access to that kind of capital as well. Many of these are the texts you need to be able to talk about, or at least bluff about convincingly enough in polite society. These are the texts the bourgeoisie hastened to read from the seventeenth century onwards because the aristocracy had been reading them, indeed claiming them as its own, and because the bourgeoisie did not want to be cut off from the company of the aristocracy, because that company would eventually provide access to the aristocracy's power, often also in exchange for the money of the bourgeoisie.

It is in the domain of cultural capital that translation can most clearly be seen to construct cultures. It does so by negotiating the passage of texts between them, or rather, by devising strategies through which texts from one culture can penetrate the textual and conceptual grids of another culture, and function in that other culture. What we call the 'socialisation process', of which formal education is a big, though not the only part, leaves us with textual and conceptual grids that regulate most of the writing and the thinking in the culture in which we grow up.

The most obvious form of negotiation between textual and conceptual grids is that of analogy; it is also the most superficial one, and the one that leads, inevitably, to the obliteration of differences between cultures and the texts they produce. Analogy is the easy way in negotiations between cultures, precisely because it slants the culture of origin toward the receiving culture, whose prestige is perceived to be so much greater. But it need not be the only way. The Schleiermacher model of translation takes issue with the automatic standardisation analogy produces. In his famous lecture 'On the Different Ways of Translating', Friedrich Schleiermacher demands, among other things, that translations from different languages into German should read and sound different: the reader should be able to guess the Spanish behind a translation from Spanish, and the Greek behind a translation from Greek. If all translations read and sound alike (as they were soon to do in Victorian translations of the classics), the identity of the source text has been lost, levelled in the target text. The Schleiermacher model emphasises the importance of 'foreignising' translation. The privileged position of the receiving language or culture is denied, and the alterity of the source text needs to be preserved.

Each of the three models referred to here has its place in a developing study of translation, as long as they are not seen (and do not see each other) as mutually exclusive. In programmes that are set up to teach the technique of translating, by which is most often meant the translating of texts that are not considered to belong to a society's cultural capital, though they are just as fundamental to that society in a different way — think of computer manuals, car manuals, medical, legal, and pharmaceutical texts — the Jerome model would have to come first, obviously, but only chronologically so. In a first stage of translation teaching, translation may still be used as a kind of proficiency check on students' knowledge of the language they are studying. Within the Jerome model students can be held to a more rigorous discipline. They can be shown where their strengths and weaknesses lie, and they can be helped to cultivate the former and overcome the latter. The Horace model needs to supplement the Jerome model in the first phase of the teaching of translating, to heighten students' awareness of the textual and conceptual grids that pre-exist the texts with which they are working.

The Horace model becomes more important on the level of the study of the actual translations of texts that can be subsumed under the category of cultural capital. It is not difficult to show how the process of negotiation, which can be said to refer to both the institutional constraints under which it took place, and the translators' own personal input, has affected the reception of certain texts in certain cultures, and how it has, at times, decisively influenced the evolution of those receptor cultures.

When juxtaposed with the Schleiermacher model, the Horace model helps us to ask the fundamental questions in the analysis of translations, questions that deal with the relative power and prestige of cultures, with matters of dominance, submission, and resistance. It should be stressed that these questions need to be answered in the translating of all kinds of texts and the analysis of all kinds of translations. The relative power and prestige of cultures is extremely relevant for the selection of texts to be translated.

Dominance shows itself in how translation changes the ways in which people write in the target culture. Advertisements written around the world now look much more like American advertisements than they did a few years ago. Submission, paradoxically, shows itself most clearly, these days, in instances of non-translation. Yuppies and would-be yuppies the world over will feel flattered by the fact that texts in their own language include the occasional English word like 'cool', or something upscale looking that ends in '-isation'. Resistance often shows itself in the refusal to accept certain aspects of the original that would lead to a negative reaction in the target culture, for instance when the original uses scantily clad models to advertise jeans and the advertising campaign is aimed at Islamic countries. Manufacturers, who want their product sold, are usually very happy to negotiate about this in the full Horatian sense of the word.

Yet, and this is perhaps the most fascinating topic right now, perhaps also because it is hardly still within the limits of any translation interfield, unless we expand once again what translation is 'felt' to be, the process of acculturation, in which translation has, traditionally, been seen as a key element, takes place not just *between cultures*, but also *inside* a given culture, any given culture. At the beginning of the socialisation process, those about to be initiated into a culture are not given access to the 'originals' of the texts that are considered to make up the cultural capital of that culture. Rather, individuals are exposed to translations of those texts, not, in most cases from another language, although, in some cases, from older stages of the same language, but literally from another world into their own: the cultural capital is rewritten in such a way that it matches their assumed level of comprehension at a certain stage in their development. These rewritings appear not just in the shape of verbal, but also of non-verbal texts. When we are deemed old enough to be exposed to some of the laws of our universe, we do not read Newton's *Principia Mathematica*, not even in some kind of translation, we are told about Newton's laws in physics textbooks. Our culture has decided that all we need from Newton now are a few formulas.

It is a sobering thought that most, if not all people who participate in a given culture will never in their life be exposed to all the 'originals' on which culture claims to be based. It is important, therefore, to realise that rewritings and translations function as originals for most, if not all people in a culture in those fields which are not an important part of their professional expertise. If fewer and fewer people read *Pride and Prejudice*, the novel, and if more and more people watch versions of it on television instead, it stands to reason that the visual rewriting of the novel will effectively replace the original, or rather, function as the original for many people.

The more the socialisation process depends on rewritings, the more the image of one culture is constructed for another by translations, the more important it becomes to know how the process of rewriting develops, and what kinds of rewritings/translations are produced. Why are certain texts rewritten/translated and not others? What is the agenda behind the production of rewritings/translations? How are the techniques of translating used in the service of a given agenda? Rewriters and translators are the people who really construct cultures on the basic level in our day and age. It is as simple, and as monumental as that. And because it is so simple and yet so monumental, it is also transparent: it tends to be overlooked.

Where Next?

And then the final question: where do we go from here? Where will Translation Studies, one of the fastest-growing interfields of the 1990s go in the new millennium? It will go in directions that we demand, as a result of our exploration of some of the as yet unresolved questions that remain to be answered.

We need to know more about the history of translation, and not just in the West, but also in other cultures. A great deal has been done, but the more we know, the more we shall be able to relativise the practices of the present, the more we shall be able to see them as constructed and contingent, not as given, eternal, and transparent.

It is no accident that so much exciting work in translation studies is coming from those cultures who are presently in a phase of post-colonial development. As the world reassesses its relationship to the European 'original', so concepts of translation are inevitably re-evaluated and canons of excellence based on Eurocentric models are revised.

We need to learn more about the acculturation process between cultures, or rather, about the symbiotic working together of different kinds of rewritings within that process, about the ways in which translation, together with criticism, anthologisation, historiography, and the production of reference works, constructs the image of writers and/or their works, and then watches those images become reality. We also *need* to know more about the ways in which one image dislodges another, the ways in which different images of the same writers and their works coexist with each other and contradict each other.

We need to learn more about the agenda behind the construction of these images: why did the Finns, for instance, suddenly decide they needed an epic? This leads us to the domain, another very promising interfield, of cultural policy, exemplified in translation and rewriting policy. Needless to say, the figure of the initiator looms large here, especially if that initiator is a (totalitarian) state, which tries to create a total image of itself with the help of the partial images it constructs. The other important factor in this respect is the relative prestige of cultures, that of Roman Antiquity versus English in Dryden's time, for instance, as compared to now, when English occupies the position of prestige language of the world.

We also need to learn more about the texts that constitute the cultural capital of other civilisations, and we need to learn about them in ways that try to overcome, or bypass the kiss of death bestowed by acculturation through analogy. Haikus are not epigrams, Chinese novels have their own rules, both the textual and conceptual grids of other civilisations should not be reduced to those of the West.

We need to find out how to translate the cultural capital of other civilisations in a way that preserves at least part of their own nature, without producing translations that are so low on the entertainment factor that they appeal only to those who read for professional reasons. Perhaps this is another area in which different forms of rewriting need to cooperate: we could imagine the translated text, translated in a way that also appeals to the non-professional reader, preceded by a long introduction which sets out to show how the original text works on its own terms, within its own grid, rather than to tell readers only what it is 'like' or even 'most like' in their own cultures. This kind of attempt is most likely to bring us up against the limits of translation, a necessary confrontation, for without such a challenge, how else are we ever to overcome such limits and move on?

Chapter 1

Chinese and Western Thinking on Translation[1]

ANDRÉ LEFEVERE

In the following pages I shall make an attempt at comparing Chinese and Western thinking about translation. Obviously, I am far more familiar with Western approaches than with Chinese thinking on the subject; what interests me mainly here, however, is translation itself. Precisely because histories of translation are increasingly being produced, we are now able to begin to historicise the phenomenon of translation itself. In consequence, we are also able to move away from the normative approach that has obstructed our view of translation for so long.

Different cultures have tended to take translation for granted, or rather, different cultures have taken the technique of translating that was current at a given time in their evolution for granted and equated it with the phenomenon of translation as such. Histories of translation in the West have shown increasingly that the technique of translating in Western cultures has changed repeatedly over the centuries, and that what was accepted as 'obvious' at one particular time was, in fact, little more than a passing phase. The important point is that shifts and changes in the technique of translating did not occur at random. Rather, they were intimately linked with the way in which different cultures, at different times, came to terms with the phenomenon of translation, with the challenge posed by the existence of the Other and the need to select from a number of possible strategies for dealing with that Other. We are, therefore, finally beginning to see different methods of translating as well as different approaches to translational practice as contingent, not eternal, as changeable, not fixed, because we are beginning to recognise that they have, indeed, changed over the centuries. Paradoxically, once it is accepted that translation is contingent, it becomes possible to highlight the central position it has always occupied in the development, indeed the very definition of cultures. That contingency is even easier to see when two different traditions are compared. Such a comparison may, I believe, shed light not just on the two traditions, but ultimately also on the phenomenon of translation itself.

In what follows I shall not discuss the activity of translating, the actual process that leads to the production of translated texts in the field delimited by the language pair Chinese and English. Rather, I shall consider what I would like to call 'translational practice' both in the Chinese and Western traditions. By translational practice I mean a practice that integrates the actual activity of translating into itself. It precedes that activity in that it gives certain guidelines, whether these are followed by particular translators or not, that are themselves the product of thinking about the process of translation within a culture. Translational practice also follows the process of translating, since it plays a part in the reception of translated texts in the culture, or cultures for which they are intended.

In short, translational practice is one of the strategies a culture devises for dealing with what we have learned to call 'the Other'. The development of a translational strategy therefore also provides good indications of the kind of society one is dealing with. The fact that China, for instance, developed translational strategies only three times in its history, with the translation of the Buddhist scriptures from roughly the second to the seventh centuries AD, with the translation of the Christian scriptures starting in the sixteenth century AD, and with the translation of much Western thought and literature starting in the nineteenth century AD, says something about the image of the Other dominant in Chinese civilisation, namely that the Other was not considered very important. Nor is China, as was sometimes erroneously believed, alone in that respect. A much more extreme example is provided by Classical Greece, which showed no interest in the Other, did not develop any thinking about translation and hardly translated anything at all.

A first and very tentative generalisation could run as follows: cultures that see themselves as central in the world they inhabit, are not likely to deal much with Others, unless they are forced to do so. The Greeks were forced to do so by the Persian invasion first, which they successfully rebuffed and could therefore afford to ignore, and then by the Roman occupation which they could ignore no longer. Yet they did not suffer much, because their language and culture were highly valued by their conquerors. The Chinese were forced to deal with the Other by the spread of Buddhism, which did not threaten the fabric of society, and therefore could be acculturated rather easily on the terms of the receiving, Chinese society. This is apparent not just from the manner of translating, but even more so from the fact that Taoist concepts were used in translations to acculturate Buddhist concepts. The story was not very different in the nineteenth century: Yan Fu and Lin Shuh could still translate into classical Chinese, following the tradition created by their predecessors, and translate on Chinese terms. Only the abolishing of classical Chinese as the language of communication between officials, literati, and intellectuals, and the concomitant rise of Western influence in China rendered this strategy of acculturation impossible in the twentieth century.

Cultures that do not pay much attention to the Other are not just cultures that consider themselves central in the great scheme of things; they are also cultures that are relatively homogeneous, as is borne out in the case of both classical Greek and Chinese cultures. Cultures that are relatively homogeneous tend to see their own way of doing things as 'naturally', the only way, which just as naturally becomes the 'best' way when confronted with other ways. When such cultures themselves take over elements from outside, they will, once again, naturalise them without too many qualms and too many restrictions. When Chinese translates texts produced by Others outside its boundaries, it translates these texts in order to replace them, pure and simple. The translations take the place of the originals. They function as the originals in the culture to the extent that the originals disappear behind the translations, not least because many of those who participated in Chinese culture did not know the language or languages of the original, which made it very difficult indeed even to check what the translators were actually doing.

The homogeneity of a culture is also a matter of the number of participants in that culture and, as importantly, a matter of how we describe that culture. Again, the similarities between Chinese and classical Greek culture are instructive in this respect. Throughout China's history, up to the beginning of this century, the number of those who really participated in the literate culture was small, which would also help to explain why it was relatively easy to maintain uniform standards for what would be acceptable to that audience, also in the matter of writing style and diction. In classical Greece, as is well known, slaves far outnumbered the free men (women were not really included) who participated in literate culture. The audiences developed differently in China and the West, however. Throughout the vagaries of history, those audiences kept expanding in the West, as opposed to China.

It should not come as much of a surprise, in the light of the above, that translation activity arose in the West in cultures that were not homogeneous, that were, in fact, internally divided by linguistic differences, or certain degrees of bilingualism. Yet in both the Western and the Chinese traditions, translation activity seems to have begun with the interpretation of spoken, rather than the translation of written texts. This is important for at least two reasons. One, though not the most important, is that translation activity does not find its origin in the translation of sacred, or even literary texts, but in the translation of oral communications that concern trade. This situation emphasises the importance of the interpreter (as we shall be calling the translator for now) as a person, as a mediator. It also stresses the importance of the actual situation in which interpretation takes place.

At the origins of translation in both traditions, communication was more direct and feedback more immediate than in later, translating situations. The important point was for both interlocutors to understand each other, and the translator/interpreter would consider his task to be accomplished successfully when that understanding had indeed taken place. Of course it was much easier for the interpreter to gauge understanding in any given situation, and it was perhaps easiest of all to do so in the situation of a commercial transaction. To accomplish his task successfully, the interpreter often could not afford to translate literally, word for word. In many cases interpreters would just convey the gist of what one partner in the conversation said to the other, they would quietly convert weights and measures, silently adjust cultural expectations. Small wonder that interpreters would, in those days as they still do now, build up a clientele based on their reputation, which would of course in turn be based on their performance. But the significant point is that the client could not really judge the quality of the performance, only its results: interpreters that helped strike a good deal were good interpreters, no matter how they might have distorted what had actually been said. Traces of this early attitude toward interpreters still lingers in Horace's famous phrase 'fidus interpres' as used in his *Ars Poetica*, where the *fidus* does not mean 'faithful to the original, or even to the wording of the original', as it has been interpreted in the light of subsequent developments, but rather something like 'dependable, someone who won't let you down'.

In this early translation process, there was not much time for correction, nor for agonising over the translation: once done, it was finished, and was seen to be transient and dependent on a particular situation. It was not etched in stone, or inscribed in clay, as it would soon be in Sumer and Akkad.

It is my contention that the Chinese and the Western tradition have developed away from the primal interpreting situation along two very different, perhaps even diametrically opposed tracks. The Chinese tradition, which I will allow to end, for the purposes of this paper, with Yan Fu and Li Shuh's nineteenth century translations has tended, on the whole, to stay closer to the interpreting situation. It has, consequently, attached comparatively less importance to the 'faithful' translation that became such a central notion in the thinking on translation that arose in the West.

The reasons why the West moved so radically away from the interpreting situation are no doubt many. In his history of translation in the West, Vermeer lists three: firstly that the society in which translation arose in the West, that of Sumer and Akkad, was bilingual to start with, not homogeneous. The Sumerian civilisation, which had flourished earlier, from about the middle of the third millennium BC, was soon (and for good around 2024 BC) overrun by the Akkadians, but for a long time afterwards Sumerian continued to be used as the language in which sacred texts were written and the language in which knowledge was communicated. The need for translation therefore became obvious. Yet translation was not easy, because Sumerian, which has not been linked to any other known language, and Akkadian, which is a Semitic language, were very different, a situation that did not obtain in the case of classical Chinese and its non-standard variants, nor in the case of the various dialects spoken in the Greece of the classical era.

Again, there is more at stake here than the difference between the two languages and the degree of difficulty in translation. Since the two languages, for all their differences, continued to be used side by side, and since Sumerian remained the prestige language, whereas Akkadian was more the language used for everyday life, the Sumerian original of the Akkadian translation never disappeared from the consciousness of the whole culture. Rather, the opposite happened: the original always remained as the timeless touchstone, the hierarchically and hieratically privileged one whenever original and translation were compared. Vermeer argues that the translation was never intended to replace the original, merely to supplement it, and then only for those who could not read the original, a fact that also contributed to the inferior social and cultural status of the translation and the translator.

However, this statement requires some modification. As long as translation took place mainly in the interpreting situation, the skills of the translator/interpreter were obviously on display, and s/he did enjoy a higher social status, not least because the fact that s/he was able to switch languages, and therefore to utter something that must have sounded akin to magical formulas to those unfamiliar with the language s/he happened to be speaking at any given moment, situated him or her if not in, at least close to the realm of magic. It is only with the rise of the concept of the faithful translation, which led to the concept of translating as transcoding, that the status of the translator fell in the West. It is easy to see why: anyone can match words from word lists. Yet from Sumer and Akkad onwards, a translation always remained what the Germans call a 'Fremdkörper', a foreign body in the receiving language, as it first was in the Akkadian language, because it was always marked as a translation, and the original always remained a foreign body in the whole culture because it remained inaccessible to a majority of those who were, after all, included in that culture.

The analogy with China is beguiling at first sight, but superficial at best, for reasons stated earlier. The real analogy is first with the European Middle Ages, and second with Europe and, gradually, the rest of the world after the Renaissance. In the Middle Ages, Latin occupied a position analogous to that of Sumerian, that of the prestige language, whereas the various national languages, then still called 'vernaculars', meaning literally 'languages of slaves', which is rather obvious in its implications about their cultural status, were in a position analogous to that of Akkadian. After the Renaissance, and in the centuries that followed, Latin was gradually superseded as a prestige language, first by French and then by English, but the basic equation remained the same, outside France and England, of course.

There is a further analogy that does bear on China, though, as well as on Sumer/Akkad and medieval and post-renaissance Europe: in each of these cultures there existed a class, or caste of literati, at first priests only, later priests and scribes and what we would now generally and generically call 'intellectuals', who had a vested interest in keeping the prestige language to themselves because it gave them access to power, and kept that power away from the vast majority of those who did not have the same access. The major difference is that whereas the Sumerian/Akkadian system collapsed after about ten centuries, and the various European systems mentioned even faster than that, the Chinese system endured much longer, surviving the collapse of discrete forms of political organisation, such as individual dynasties, and maintaining itself in power until the beginning of the twentieth century.

One might say that whereas the Chinese system that ensured the political and cultural dominance of the prestige language lasted until the beginning of the twentieth century in a more or less intact form, until it suddenly collapsed from within, attempts to realise a similar system in the West met with progressively more and more limited success. Even though the Roman Catholic Church tried to ensure that the Bible, its sacred text, would be available only in Latin in Western Europe, partial translations of it in several national languages already appeared around the year 1000, eroding the dominance of Latin. Successor prestige languages such as French and English did not have the power to limit their own distribution to anywhere near the same extent as classical Chinese.

In Sumer/Akkad translation was assisted by the fact that both languages used the same writing system: the cuneiform system invented by the Sumerians. The same sign sequence would signify 'house' in both Sumerian and in Akkadian, but in Sumerian it would be pronounced *gal* and in Akkadian it would be pronounced *bitu*. Similarly, the number 5 is, to this day, pronounced *wu* in Mandarin Chinese and *ng* in Cantonese.

Yet precisely the existence of this common writing system leads us indirectly to the first reason given by Vermeer as to why the West moved away so radically from the interpreting situation: the emergence of the word as the unit of translation. Vermeer links that emergence to the compilation of word lists in Sumer/Akkad. Because of the bilingual nature of Sumero-Akkadian culture these word lists were naturally bilingual, and they were compiled centuries before Hsü Shu's *Shuo-wen*, the first Chinese dictionary. Even though these word lists were limited to words used in rituals and words needed for the transmission of knowledge, the very fact of their compilation, Vermeer suggests, was enough to focus attention on the word in the sense just mentioned.

Yet it was not so much the emergence of the word as the unit of translation that was responsible for the radical split between Chinese and Western thinking on translation, as the concomitant decontextualisation of that word. Once the word is written and once it can be equated with another word, once it can, in fact, be abstracted from an actual situation in which two interlocutors converse through a translator/interpreter, that translator may well be content with just matching words, no matter whether they will fit their new situation or not, the more so since he will not have to contend with any immediate feedback from his interlocutors, who are now absent, and will, at best, criticise the translation (much) later, a factor which will also lessen the impact of that feedback on the translator.

Vermeer suggests that a second reason for the emergence of faithfulness as the dominant criterion of translation in Western thinking about the subject is to be found in the identification of the grammatical unit 'word', as discovered in Sumer/Akkad with the Platonic concept of the 'logos', no doubt aided and abetted by the fact that the grammatical unit 'word' was also referred to as 'logos' in classical Greek. In Vermeer's words: 'What was expressed by means of the word was posited "objectively" as an invariable object, as the *tertium comparationis* (the third, middle element in the comparison), which was the same beyond all individual languages. Translation therefore became linguistic transcoding' (Vermeer, 1992).

In the West translation became much more of a linguistic transcoding independent of a particular situation and with little regard for a particular readership than it ever became in China, where what Vermeer calls 'functionally thinking rhetoric' (Vermeer, 1992) remains much stronger. Chinese translators did translate with a certain audience in mind, and they would rhetorically adapt their translations to that audience. Perhaps the most arresting negative illustration of this practice is to be found in Yan Fu's famous statement that if people who had not read the Chinese classics were to read his translations, they would not understand them, but that 'was the fault of the readers and the translator is not to blame' (Vermeer, 1992), because those readers are not the readers for whom the translator rhetorically shaped his translation. Significantly, the fact that those readers exist is indicative of a widening of the audience beyond what had existed for so many centuries.

The Platonic logos, then, decisively devalued what the rhetoric of Western Classical Antiquity, which plays a rather large part in Vermeer's book, referred to in Greek as *'to prepon'*, 'that which is fitting to a given situation', implying that there is no 'absolute' truth, that the truth is always, at least to some extent, dependent on the situation at hand or, to put it in more linguistic terms, that although words may have meanings that can be fixed in word lists, these words acquire their actual meanings only in a given situation.

The West's fixation on the word was further reinforced by another transformation of the Platonic logos, from abstract to anthropomorphic, when what was the abstract 'tertium comparationis' became merged with the Hebrew Yahweh and the Christian God came into being.

It cannot be emphasised enough that like His Hebrew counterpart, the Christian God has both His lenient and His less lenient sides, which means His wrath is not to be trifled with, least of all by translators trying to translate His own words as written down in the holy scriptures. The ultimate power with which the Western translator of holy scriptures has to contend is therefore God Himself, and the power He has is not just a power of life and death, but a power that goes even beyond death itself and can give salvation or damnation. Needless to say, the ultimate presence behind the Buddhist holy scriptures, the Buddha himself, is very different from the Christian God in this respect. This may also go some way in explaining why Chinese thinking about translation is less beset with anxiety and guilt feelings than its Western counterpart. Early on, translators of the Buddhist scriptures learned to live with the fact that their translations were done by mortals and would therefore of necessity be imperfect. We do not find anywhere near the same sense of equanimity in Western thinking on translation.

Eusebius Hieronymus (St. Jerome), his predecessors and his detractors all firmly believed that the scriptures they were translating were inspired by God himself, were therefore true beyond all dispute, and should be rendered into the target language ideally unchanged, and in practice with as little change as possible. If taken at face value, as it was for a long time in the West, certainly in the translation of the Bible which became, in turn, the touchstone for all other kinds of translation, this requirement amounts to an impossible demand.

This may explain why so many prefaces to translations in the Western tradition are fundamentally apologetic in tone. Translator after translator begins by stating that the task ahead is impossible and then proceeds to apologise profusely for not being able to perform this impossible task.

Because of this fundamental opposition between the two traditions, Chinese thinking about translation is able to historicise its originals in ways Western thinking about translation was never able to, as long as translation of the Bible was kept in the theological sphere. No statement in the early stages of the Western tradition is able to echo Dao'an's statement to the effect that 'the Saint must preach in deference to the conventions of his time. The conventions change with time' (Book 55, 52).

For the same reason, it would have been literally inconceivable for St. Jerome to emulate the strategy Chinese translators of the Buddhist scriptures used from the days of Zhi Qian onwards, namely to borrow concepts from Laotzu to acculturate Buddhist concepts into Chinese, even though other Church Fathers had done something very similar before him, namely to achieve a (what they hoped would be) balanced mixture between the emerging teachings of Christianity, as formulated by Paul as much as by Christ himself, and the basic tenets of Greek philosophy with which they had been familiar from childhood onwards. They were able to do so in the form of a commentary, a treatise, or any other form of writing *about* the text, but they would not have dreamed of doing so in the shape of translation, which can be seen to alter the text, especially not once the canon of the Bible had been established, not long before Dao'an established the canon of the Buddhist scriptures in Chinese.

Of course I am not suggesting that any translator in the West who now happens to translate either poetry or a computer manual does so with an image of a wrathful God in his or her mind's eye, nor am I suggesting that her or his Chinese counterpart feels more relaxed while performing the same task because she or he is confident the Buddha will ultimately be kind, before or after death. What I am suggesting, though, is that these attitudes were among several factors that are to be found at the origin of thinking on translation in both China and the West, that they have been formative influences on the traditions of thinking about translation, and that they live on, however secularised, in much thinking about translation today.

Let us now take a closer look at the translation of scriptures, in China and the West, namely at the translation of Buddhist scriptures into Chinese and at the translation of the Bible into Latin from Greek and Hebrew sources by Saint Jerome.

Starting with the method of translation, the first obvious difference between the two enterprises is to be found in the fact that when the Buddhist scriptures were first translated into Chinese, there were hardly any written texts available, and those available might just as easily be written in Central Asian and Indic languages as in Sanskrit. The language in which they were written is of less importance than the glaring fact that this medium of transmitting the scriptures was inseparably bound up with what I have called the interpreting situation, even though the texts that were recited were also actually written down in the *koushou* stage of the interpreting process. Jerome, on the other hand, worked from written documents and found himself in the translation situation from the start. Obviously the distinction did not remain as clear cut: written texts of the Buddhist scriptures became gradually available for translation into Chinese, but my contention is, once again, that the first attempt at doing something is bound to establish a tradition, and that these traditions are one of the causes of the difference between thinking about translation in China and the West.

Perhaps the most striking difference between the two traditions is that of the faithfulness/freedom opposition in translation, which has plagued Western thinking on the subject virtually from Cicero onwards, only to be exacerbated by the translation of the holy scriptures, and which appears to be largely absent from the Chinese tradition. Of course the first translations of the Buddhist scriptures into Chinese were done in what was referred to as a 'simple' style, or *wen*, but mainly because the early Buddhist missionaries, such as An Shigao, a Parthian, and Zhi Loujiachan, a Scythian, who translated those scriptures were not all that well-versed in Chinese.

Perhaps the supreme irony revealed by a comparison between the two ways of thinking about translation is that the *wen* style, abandoned by Chinese translators after one, or at most two generations, is analogous to the style adopted by Eusebius Hieronymus in his translation of the Vulgate, a translation full of transliterations from Hebrew, and syntactic constructions closely modelled on Greek and, to a lesser extent, Hebrew, precisely the two translational features that vanished from translations into Chinese as soon as these translations were mainly done by Chinese themselves, roughly from the time of Zhi Qian onward. After Zhi Qian, translations were done in the elegant style, or *zhi*, suitable for literary production, no doubt because the translators realised that was the only style that would be taken seriously by the target audience of officials, literati, and intellectuals. This remained the style for translation until classical Chinese was replaced by spoken Chinese also as the language of communication among those elite groups at the beginning of the twentieth century.

Another striking difference between the two traditions that becomes immediately obvious is that the Chinese tradition emphasises what we would now call teamwork, while the Western tradition has often frowned upon that very concept. It is well known that the early translations of Buddhist scriptures into Chinese were produced in three distinct stages. The first stage, *koushou*, was that of oral interpretation of the text, which was often written down only during the process of interpreting. The second stage, *chuanyan*, was that of oral instruction, transmission, and recitation. The third stage, *bishou*, was that of enscribing in Chinese. From the very beginning, then, translation in China was not the lonely pursuit it has mainly been in the West. In fact, the teamwork was later institutionalised, with twelve different people holding twelve different titles and doing twelve different types of work.

It is well known that Jerome also worked with a group of helpers, since he surrounded himself in his Bethlehem retreat with monks and noble Roman ladies, but it is doubtful that he ever had at his disposal a number of assistants anywhere near to the 800 Kumarajiva is reported to have had. As far as we can reconstruct what went on in Jerome's Bethlehem equivalent of the 'Carefree Garden' that was established in Chang'an under the patronage of Fu Jian, three years before Jerome started his work on translating the Bible, he used his assistants more as walking dictionaries than as partners in the actual composition of the translated text.

It would be misleading in the extreme to suggest that the differences between Chinese and Western thinking on translation can be reduced to a mere matter of method. There is also, perhaps more importantly, although one should not underestimate the impact of a tradition once it is established, the matter of the role the translated text is to play in the receiving culture. In Chinese culture that matter was resolved relatively early on, as stated above, and once it was resolved there was little or no looking back. The new text, the translation, was destined to function in the receiving culture in the place of the old text, and function it would, whether it had been perfectly translated or not.

In the Chinese tradition, moreover, at least since Zhi Qian, form was always as important as content, with the even more important proviso, though, that the form of the translation was to be a Chinese form, not a form that tried to carry across even a suggestion of the form of the original. That only began to happen when the Chinese tradition was coming to an end. Only then did poets like Feng Chi begin to try to naturalise the Western form of the sonnet, for instance, in Chinese.

In the Western tradition, on the other hand, form has routinely been thought less important than content, especially in the case of the translation of holy scripture, where the Chinese concept of *ya*, or elegance, never played a significant part. The concept of *ya* never became dominant in the Western tradition because in that tradition a translation is not supposed to replace another text, at least not in the sense of obliterating it; rather the text, the original, always remains as a presence behind or beyond the translation: it is always there as a touchstone and, even more significantly, it is invested with the ultimate authority. In other words, the translation never really stands as a text on its own, with rare exceptions, and the translator always has to look over his or her shoulder at the original. This situation also explains why texts were and are retranslated frequently in the West, or rather in the different Western traditions, unless certain translations are sanctioned to be treated as near originals.

This is precisely what happened to Jerome's translation (which was itself also partly a revision of previously produced translations) of the Bible into Latin, which became known as the Vulgate, and which was proclaimed the official version of the Roman Catholic Bible. Such sanctioning by power further reinforces the ambiguous status of the translation, which may be elevated to the position of an original, even if it is, basically, a translation. This also explains why translation has been so tightly constrained and circumscribed in the West, precisely because it was also seen as the potential Achilles heel of power. What if the translation that serves as the foundation narrative of a culture actually turns out to be untenable, at least in places? Such mistakes could be liable to undermine the foundations of power itself. Small wonder that the Roman Catholic Church tried to discourage (by intimidation) and prevent (by coercion and execution) both translations from the Vulgate into the different national languages of Europe, or revisions of the Vulgate itself for at least ten centuries, even though it was never completely successful in doing so.

Power obviously also played a role in the translation of the Buddhist scriptures into Chinese. We are reminded of Dao'an's statement to the effect that 'the case of Buddhism will go nowhere without the support of the monarch'. As opposed to what happened in the West, however, the translation of Buddhist scriptures lost its official patronage in China about three hundred years later, while official support for the Vulgate, at least on the part of the Roman Catholic Church, continues to this day. In practice, the Vulgate remained unchallenged until the sixteenth century, when Erasmus published his translation of the New Testament, and then only with the proviso that his translation should only be read by scholars and that the Vulgate should remain the translation in general use.

Early Western translations of the Bible into the different national languages of Europe historicise their original only when they step outside the realms of theology and into those of literature. When they do not pretend to be translations in the strict sense of transcodings, as Vermeer calls them, they become retellings or 'biblical epics' as they are called in histories of both Old

English and Old High German literature. Here the analogy with the Chinese tradition becomes clear again, as it often does when compared to those elements of the Western tradition that never achieved dominance, or whose dominance was relatively short-lived. Perhaps the closest a variant of the Western tradition ever came to the Chinese tradition was during the relatively short period during which the *'Belles Infidèles'* type of translation was dominant in France. To be sure, that type of translation only became dominant outside the religious/theological sphere, but its dominance rested on an attitude similar to that prevalent in the Chinese tradition, namely that of positing its own culture as central and, concomitantly, of acculturating the Other on its own terms only. The ideal of the unchanged translation of the word of God, because it is the word of God, still lives on in the West in the concept of the faithful translation.

What can such a comparison as I have been trying to make show us about the phenomenon of translation as such? The first, and most obvious point, is that translation spans a field immeasurably wider than that which involves the mere technical activity of translating. Or, to put it in starker terms: language only has a tangential impact on translation; at best it can be equated with transcoding. Rather, the factors that shape how a culture defines translation for itself seem to be language-independent but still culturally bound to a great extent. These factors include power, whether wielded by the Roman Catholic Church or the emperors of the Han, Sui, or T'ang dynasties, the self-image of a culture and the degree to which a culture may be homogeneous or not, and, perhaps the strongest of them all, although I am reluctant to admit it after this longish exercise in comparative genealogy, contingency: what, we may well ask, would have happened if the Chinese translators of the Buddhist scriptures had had written texts to work with from the outset?

Note

1. I am very much indebted to two people for what follows. One is my German colleague Hans J. Vermeer, whose very erudite and somewhat idiosyncratic history of translation, which is what he calls his history of translation in the West, has made me think, and in some cases think again about many fundamental issues connected with the topic at hand. The other is my former graduate student Yan Yang, late from Shanghai, and at present working in Austin, whose doctoral dissertation on Chinese thinking about translation has provided me with new insights.

References

Vermeer, Hans J. (1992) *Skizzen zu einer Geschicte der Translation*. Frankfurt/M: Verlag für interkulterelle Kommunikation. 2 volumes.

Chapter 2

When is a Translation Not a Translation?

SUSAN BASSNETT

Recent debates on translation have focused more and more on exploring the relationship between what is termed 'translation' and what is termed 'original'. Those debates are, inevitably, also linked to questions of authority and power. One line of thought has traditionally seen the translation as a traducement, a betrayal, an inferior copy of a prioritised original. Another line of thinking focuses instead on the translation, and in recent years we have seen Derrida (and others) rereading Walter Benjamin and celebrating the translation as the 'after-life' of the source text, its means of survival, its reincarnation. Indeed, Derrida suggests that effectively the translation *becomes* the original (Derrida, 1985). This view is entirely credible if we think of the terms in which most readers approach a translated text. When we read Thomas Mann or Homer, if we have no German or Ancient Greek, what we are reading is the original through translation, i.e. that translation is our original.

The shift of emphasis from original to translation is reflected also in discussions on the visibility of the translator. Lawrence Venuti calls for a translator-centred translation, insisting that the translator should inscribe him/herself visibly into the text (Venuti, 1995). Barbara Godard argues that a feminist translator should 'flaunt' the signs of her manipulation of the text, her 'woman-handling' strategies (Godard, 1990). Not that such views are wildly radical; after all, it is precisely what translators have been doing for centuries. We have only to think of Chapman's extraordinary manipulation of Homer in the sixteenth century, or de la Motte's version of the same a century later, to see that translators of the past have had no difficulty in inscribing themselves very firmly into their own translations. Despite protestations to the contrary, many translators have deliberately chosen to assert themselves very visibly indeed in the texts they produce.

Borges' absurd story, 'Pierre Menard, author of the *Quixote*' serves as a salutary reminder of the impossibility of a translation ever being identical to an original (Borges, 1964). Borges' protagonist aims to write his own version of *Don Quixote* in the twentieth century, and the story relates how he sets about doing this. Since he wants to recreate the identical text, he has to live out an identical life to that of the original author. This involves reliving Cervantes' life in every detail, since only in this way can he ever hope to succeed. In the story, he does succeed, and writes a novel identical in every word to the original.

The story of Pierre Menard illustrates the absurdity of any concept of sameness between texts. Borges never uses the word 'translation', but his story is about translation all the same. Pierre Menard's ridiculous proposition is as foolish as that of a translator who believes that he or she can reproduce an identical equivalent text in another language. What actually happens, is that the signs of the translator's involvement in the process of interlingual transfer will always be present, and those signs can be decoded by any reader examining the translation process

The new discipline, or preferably interdiscipline of translation studies has battled for space between literary studies, linguistics, and the social sciences, and in the course of the struggles it has undergone many changes. From a phase in which it was fighting for recognition, translation studies is now at a point where it has a chameleon quality, able to change its colour and shape, to translate itself into many different things. And inevitably so, for lines that may once have seemed clear are now blurred and difficult to decipher. When the subject was born, in the early 1970s, the Cold War was still in existence, albeit thawing a little, the Pacific Rim countries had yet to rise to economic supremacy globally, the Vietnam war was still being fought, the European Union was establishing itself — one could go on ad infinitum pointing out the great differences between that time and our own. The 1970s were a different world. We had yet to discover the video, let alone the Internet. So the early debates about translation were still, in many ways, the same debates that had been going on for most of the century, debates about faithfulness and equivalence and the meaning of cultural difference. We are now at a watershed in translation studies, where there are all kinds of shifting and conflicting concepts of translation being continually reassessed and revised. Since there is no longer any consensus of approaches to the subject (if indeed there ever was!), it is important to consider whether there is a consensus of expectations. And here I introduce a term that does not normally enter into discussions about translation. That term is collusion.

Colluding with the Text

When we collude with something, we go along with it, we agree with it, but only to a certain point. In violent domestic relationships there is often some degree of collusion between partners: it is collusion that makes it so very difficult for psychotherapists to sort out clearly 'right' from 'wrong' in absolute terms. And we all collude with things in different ways. Probably none of us lives out a life of limpidly clear moral choices every day that are unproblematised. There is, following on from this, such a thing as collusion between readers and writers, to which some literary theorists have drawn our attention. Roland Barthes, for example, invited us to reconsider the role and power of the author in the making of a text:

> The text is a tissue of quotations drawn from the innumerable centres of culture ... (the author's) only power is to mix writings, to counter the ones with the others, in such a way as never to rest on any one of them ...(Barthes, 1977)

Barthes's essay on the death of the author both infuriated and exhilarated readers. Some, following in the footsteps of Harold Bloom, were anxious about influence all along and could not countenance the idea of free textuality along Barthean lines. But is he really saying anything so very radical, when we look at this essay today? Isn't it obvious that all texts are a tissue of quotations, for how can anything be truly 'original' unless it has been created by someone who has never encountered anyone else's work? Of course Emily Dickinson's poetry is startling and wonderful and we call it 'original', but although she may have been something of a recluse, Emily Dickinson had read all sorts of texts and fragments and echoes of all she read drift through her poems. We can trace literary echoes in the works of all writers. In the same way, no two translations are going to be alike, as we all know, because fragments of our individualistic readings will drift through our reading and our translating. Difference is built into the translation process, both on the levels of the readerly and the writerly.

Turning to address the question of when a translation may not be a translation, the term 'collusion' will serve us well. For as readers, we collude with the usages of that term 'translation', a term that distinguishes one type of textual practice from others. By pretending that we know what translation is, i.e. an operation that involves textual transfer across a binary divide, we tie ourselves up with problems of originality and authenticity, of power and ownership, of dominance and subservience. But can we always be certain that we know what a translation is? and is the object we call a translation always the same kind of text?

Pseudotranslation

In an important essay, Gideon Toury discusses 'pseudotranslation', the text that claims falsely to be a translation. Some writers, Toury points out, resort to the term 'translation' to describe a text that they have created from scratch themselves. He argues that the use of what he calls 'fictitious translations' is often a convenient way of introducing innovations into a literary system, 'especially when this system is resistant to deviations from canonical models and norms' (Toury, 1985). The classic example of this kind of fictitious translation is Macpherson's 18th century version of the poetry of Ossian, which he claimed to have translated and which was a huge success right across Europe in the aftermath of the French Revolution. The impact of Macpherson's pseudotranslation in several literatures was extensive, despite his relative obscurity in the English literary tradition.

Toury also points out that the phenomenon of pseudotranslation is not so rare as it may seem, although in modern literature it tends to be marginal rather than occupying a canonical position. Toury's concern in his essay is with the identification of norms, and he comments:

> If, in such cases, translational norms differ from the norms of original literary writing in the target culture, and if the difference is in the direction of greater tolerance for deviations from sanctioned models, as is often the case, then the translational norms can also be adopted, at least in part, for the composition of original texts, which are introduced into the system in the guise of genuine translations and, as a result, have a lower resistance threshold to pass.

The pseudotranslation, Toury contends, gives us an idea of the generally accepted notions of those characteristics that determine a translation which are held by the target language community at a given time. For in seeking to convince readers that the pseudotranslation is a genuine translation, its author has to take into account the expectations of the potential readership. Toury goes on to make a distinction between *translations of literary texts* and *literary translation*, arguing that despite some overlap, these texts are produced via different methods and with different aims, so that in consequence the questions they pose to scholars will necessarily be different.

Following on from Toury, it is apparent that the fictitious translation is a long established convention, and variations of this device deserve more critical attention than they have so far received. Borges' Pierre Menard story is made doubly absurd when we recall that Cervantes himself used the device of the fictitious translation in his novel. It is also the case that, as readers, we collude with an idea of translation in all kinds of diverse reading practices. This essay will consider, briefly, some of those reading practices and look at different types of pseudotranslations.

The Inauthentic Source

Thomas Mallory's *Morte d'Arthur* was printed by Caxton in 1485. In his Preface, Caxton explains that there was a proliferation of Arthurian material in French, Welsh and some in English, but that he commissioned Mallory to make a new text:

> Wherefore, such as have late been drawn out briefly into English, I have after the simple cunning that God hath sent to me, under the favour and correction of all noble lords and gentlemen, emprised to imprint a book of the noble histories of the said King Arthur and of certain of his knights, after a copy unto me delivered, which copy Sir Thomas Mallory did take out of certain books of French, and reduced it into English.

Note the word 'reduced', a curious term in this context. What exactly is Caxton saying that he has agreed to print? Is it a translation, a compilation, or something else ? And does it matter? It certainly didn't matter either to the author (if he can be called that), the printer or the readers when it first appeared. The *Morte d'Arthur* is a text that is a retelling of a body of narrative material. It is a rewriting, and at this juncture we should recall that Andre Lefevere increasingly called for translations to be retermed 'rewritings', in order to both raise the status of the translator and get away from the limitations of the term 'translation. '

If we look at the high point of this huge work, the actual death of Arthur, we find something very curious. Arthur has been wounded in the battle against Mordred and Sir Bedevere is the sole witness of Arthur's passing, as he is born away in a barge by three ladies. One might expect a long description of Arthur's last moments, but instead the narrative deals with his end almost summarily:

> Thus of Arthur I find never more written in books that be authorised, nor more of the very certainty of his death heard I never read, but thus was he led away in a ship wherein were three queens; ... More of the death of Arthur could I never find, but that ladies brought him to his burials; and such one was buried there, that the hermit bore witness that sometime was Bishop of Canterbury, but yet the hermit knew not in certain that he was verily the body of King Arthur; for this tale Sir Bedevere, knight of the Table Round, made it to be written.

This is a fascinating passage: the author seems to be claiming that he drew upon several sources for his account, and seems to be suggesting that those sources were somehow 'authentic'. But he also claims that Sir Bedevere, a fictional character, caused the tale to be written. Which tale is he talking about? The story of the death of Arthur that he has just claimed came from different sources? The text he is writing? Is he claiming a new authentic source, one that can be ultimately attributed to Bedevere? And what an extraordinary way to end a narrative that has been building up to the title, the morte (death) of Arthur. Mallory claims authentic sources and yet deliberately blurs all traces that might lead us back to those sources. And we, as readers collude with this, because it is a quintessential story-telling device. It is the same device that Henry James uses in *The Turn of the Screw*, for example, when the narrator narrates how he was told a story by someone who was told that story by the governess who is the protagonist of the narrative. It is the device that Borges uses again and again in his short stories, deliberately questioning the notion of an absolute truth or unimpeachable source.

So let us argue that the literary device of the supposed source that the reader can never verify is a classic one that has survived across the centuries and is indeed a powerful convention, used in detective fiction or the horror story all the time, as a device to increase the reader's sense of insecurity. In the *Morte d'Arthur* this device is used both as a frame for the entire narrative and within that narrative itself. The reader both knows and does not know that Mallory was not translating anything, What happens is that we collude from the outset with the printer's claims that Malory started with an authoritative source and then we allow the author to manipulate us through the stages of the narrative, even in extremis with the death of the hero.

The idea of the authentic source or original that exists outside the text is a standard story-telling device. Claims that a text may be a translation are another variant of this, and Mallory's epic work assumes that readers will be aware of the body of material about Arthur that existed in several languages and travelled backwards and forwards across Europe. The question is, however, whether we may call this kind of text a translation, for although it presupposes an original somewhere else and claims to be a rendering of that original, the original is not a single text but a body of material in several languages.

Self-translation

The phenomenon of so-called self-translation introduces another dimension to the question of when a translation may or may not be a translation. Samuel Beckett famously wrote in both French and English, claiming at times to have translated his own texts. His sequence of four short poems, *Quatre poèmes* (1961), is published with the French and English versions on facing pages. The fact that the French is printed on the left hand page signals that the poems were first written in that language. A note informs the reader that the poems have been translated from the French by the author.

The differences between the English and French versions of these poems are fascinating, but for the purposes of this essay, I will focus on one line only. The fourth poem in the sequence, 'je voudrais que mon amour meure', is a four line text. The first line expresses the poet's wish for his love to die, the second line presents the image of rain falling on a graveyard, the third line extends this to the streets in which the poet walks and the fourth line moves back to the dead love, but in strikingly different ways. The French version reads: 'pleurant celle qui crut m'aimer', while the English is 'mourning the first and last to love me. ' The meaning of the two lines in the two languages is completely different. Is the English therefore a translation? The last line appears to be not just a rewriting but a complete rethinking of the original concept.

The edition in which these poems appear states explicitly that the English version is a translation. But given the difference in meaning, can we attribute any authority at all to the 'original'? We might also question whether there is an original, for surely the printing of these two versions side by side means that we read both these texts and grapple with the dialectical relationship between them. If they were published separately, we could perfectly well read just one of them and be satisfied. But the moment we are told that the English is a translation of the French, we are thrown up against the problem of the 'authenticity' of the 'original'. One solution to the dilemma is to deny the existence of any original here, and consequently to deny the existence of a translation, assuming instead that we have two versions of the same text that simply happen to have been written by the same author in different languages.

Inventing a Translation

Let us turn now to another case that highlights the difficulty of defining translation. In 1880, Bernard Quaritch published *The Kasidah of Hají Abdú El-Yezdí*. The title page states that the text has been translated and annotated by the friend and pupil of the author, one F.B. A Preface, addressed to the reader claims that the text 'aims at being in advance of its time', and points out that details concerning both the poem and its author are given at the end of the volume.

Those details are copious in the extreme. The poem itself occupies 58 pages and there are a further 40 pages of notes. The last paragraph of the notes reads as follows:

Here ends my share of the work. On the whole it has been considerable.

I have omitted, as has been seen, sundry stanzas, and I have changed the order of others. The text has nowhere been translated verbatim; in fact a familiar European turn has been given to many sentiments which were judged to be too Oriental. As the metre adopted by Hají Abdú was the _Bahr Tawil_ (long verse), I thought it advisable to preserve that peculiarity, and to fringe it with the rough, unobtrusive rhyme of the original. Vive, valeque! (F.B., 1880)

Now the text has indeed nowhere been translated verbatim, because it has never been translated at all. F. B. is none other than Richard Francis Burton, the translator, explorer, early anthropologist (and sexologist) and one of the most gifted linguists of his day. The poem was published under the initials of F.B. (Frank Baker, his alter-ego) in 1880, the same year that also saw the publication of his translation of the Portuguese epic, _The Lusiads_. He became so involved in this translation project, that the following year he published a two volume study of the author, Camões, and a commentary on the poem. Given that he was a prodigious translator, why did he choose to conceal his identity as writer of the Kasidah and go to such lengths to invent a fictitious persona for himself, including such detailed notes?

His wife, Isobel, claimed he wrote this 'masterpiece', as she describes it in her Preface to the 1894 edition, in 1853, after his return from Mecca. If this were true, then he would have written it a good four years before Fitzgerald's hugely popular _Rubaiyat of Omar Khayham_ came out. Burton, not Fitzgerald, would then have been seen as the man who introduced Persian mysticism to English readers. But Frank McLynn, Burton's biographer does not believe this for a moment. He claims that the 'supremely mendacious Isobel' went to great lengths to conceal the fact that Burton wrote his text in 1880, and argues that there are textual echoes of his Camoeñs translation, besides traces of Confucius, Longfellow, Aristotle, Pope, Das Kabir, Palumbal and, of course, Fitzgerald (McLynn, 1990). He suggests that Burton's 'elaborate charade' was simply because 'he felt that the Kasidah would be weighed in the balance alongside the Rubaiyat and found wanting'. Fitzgerald, at the end of the day, was a better poet than Burton.

It is difficult to decide exactly how to categorise this text. It could be termed a pseudotranslation, though the objective does not appear to have been to introduce innovation into the target system. It could be described as a literary forgery, but that does not seem adequate either. What we have is a writer who spent a lifetime translating texts from a range of different languages, and who tried his hand at writing a text that could not be written from within his own literary system. It had to be seen to be a translation, because otherwise it would have no place in the English system. This might mean that it could be termed an imitation, but the extensive notes, which are not in any way ironic and are to be taken seriously, appear to be included to grant greater authenticity to the poem. Burton seems to have used the device of the fictitious translation both to grant greater status to the poem and also to allow him to write in a way that the English literary system would not have permitted. Calling it a translation also enabled him to include the detailed notes that he seems to have enjoyed writing most. He would hardly have been able to provide a similar annotation system to his own writing. He had to pretend that he was someone other than the creator of his own text in order to present that text in the way he wanted.

Travellers as Translators

The enormous success of travel literature, particularly in the English-speaking world, is increasingly the object of study. Post-colonial scholarship has drawn attention to the implicit imperialist discourse in a great deal of travel literature, for travel writers create their portraits of other cultures explicitly for home consumption, thereby setting them up as the Other. While an account of a journey may seem to be innocent, there is always an ideological dimension, for the traveller is approaching his or her material from a particular perspective, the perspective of the outsider (for the time and space of the journey) writing for an inside group back home. Madan Sarup, following on from Edward Said, sums up the contradiction inherent in travel writing:

> On the one hand, it is interesting to leave one's homeland in order to enter the culture of others but, on the other hand, this move is undertaken only to return to oneself and one's home, to judge or to laugh at one's peculiarities and limitations. In other words, the foreigner becomes the figure on to which the penetrating, ironical mind of the philosopher is delegated — his double, his mask. (Sarup, 1994)

One particularly fascinating aspect of the complexities of decoding travel writing is the role occupied by translation. Since the texts are written for a readership that may be assumed not to have the same access to the culture being described, linguistic difference is signalled in the text. So, for example, one common device is the use of pidgin English. In Redmond O'Hanlon's account of the journey he and James Fenton undertook to the mountains of Borneo, the local guides speak an English that is clearly the product of the writer's over-heated imagination, as this passage shows:

'Leon, what the hell are these things?'

'Very good', said Leon, 'we save them in salts till we reach this far place. They the little snakes that live in the fishes. How you say it?'
'Jesus!' I said. 'worms'.
'Jesus worms', said Leon, 'very good'.
(O'Hanlon, 1984)

The intention here is to create a comic picture of two Europeans forced to deal with the horrors of unfamiliar food, a classic component of much travel writing. But the English is bizarre, and appears to be a kind of invented language that is meant to signal the foreignness of the speaker. This device, patronising in the extreme, is meant to convey a sense of authenticity to the dialogue, reminding the reader that the speaker is using a non-standard form of English. The likelihood of it being an authentic transcription of the English used by a native of Borneo is, however, doubtful.

Elsewhere in travel writing, dialogues may contain similar indices of foreignness, or they may be written in standard English that presupposes some kind of translation. Frequently, travel writers recount dialogues that they claim have taken place between themselves and inhabitants of other lands. In some cases, travellers cross a great many borders and encounter speakers of some dozen or more languages, all of which are transcribed in English. Moreover, travellers in isolated places obviously encounter dialect speakers, and some pride themselves on conversations with road sweepers, camel drivers and peasant grandmothers. The question then arises as to which language the dialogue is supposed to represent.

Robert Byron's classic account of the journey he undertook with his companion, Christopher, in search of early Islamic architecture in Persia and Afghanistan, *The Road to Oxiana*, uses all kinds of strategies to signal that dialogues have been in some way translated. Sometimes he uses pidgin English, elsewhere he signals that the speaker knew English and so transcribes the dialogue in standard English, in one case he keeps a dialogue in French. But there are also all kinds of dialogues that are written in standard English but appear to have taken place in another language. One such example comes during a visit to a mosque in Meshed. The two men have taken pains to disguise themselves and stain their faces. Christopher, however, has a light coloured beard, and the guide devises a way for him to conceal it:

'Please blow your nose', whispered our guide to Christopher.
'Why?'
'I ask you, blow it, and continue to blow it. You must cover your beard'
(Byron, 1937)

Obeying the orders of their guide, who addresses them in the language of an English headmaster, the two men enter the court. The guide gives them further instructions, in the same headmasterly tone:

> 'Now', hissed our guide, 'we are coming to the main gate. I shall talk to you, Mr Byron, when we go out. You, Mr Sykes, please blow your nose and walk behind'. Guards, porters and ecclesiastics stood up respectfully as they saw him come. He seemed entirely preoccupied with his own conversation, which took the form of a charwoman's monologue, and sounded so remarkable in Persian that I had no need to simulate interest. 'So I said to him rumble rumble rumble rumble Rumble he said rumble Rumble? I said I said and rumble rumble Rumble rumble he said to me I said Rumble! rumblerumblerumblerumble ...' Everyone bowed. Our guide cast an eye over his shoulder to see that Christopher was following and we were out, got a cab, and were soon scrubbing our faces at the hotel before returning to the Consulate.

The reader may well wonder what is going on here. Is the guide speaking in English, perfect English at that, despite being in a dangerous situation where he is seeking to disguise the two Englishmen? And when he speaks in Persian, which he presumably does to deceive the guards, porters and ecclesiastics watching, what can we deduce about the author's understanding of what he says? In short, how truthful can we take this kind of dialogue to be?

Authenticity, the truthful account by a traveller of what he or she sees, is presented as a fundamental element of travel writing. Readers are invited to share an experience that has actually happened. When we read a travel account, we do not expect to read a novel; rather we assume that the author will be documenting his or her experiences in another culture. But the dialogues are so often patently invented that authenticity begins to dissolve. We could say that one of the bases upon which travel writing rests, is the collusion of writer and reader in a notion of authenticity, that is, the reader agrees to suspend disbelief and go along with the writer's pretence.

In 1990, William Dalrymple brought out his own account of a journey across Central Asia, *In Xanadu: A Quest*. Following in the footsteps of Byron, Dalrymple recounts how he and his girl-friend travelled across various borders and gives details of several comic dialogues with officials and police. At one point, in Saveh in Iran, he recounts how he persuaded a policeman to trust him by showing his Cambridge University library card, which so impressed the foreign official that he cut through all red tape. This kind of anecdote, very much in the tradition of comic imperialist writing, is presented as authentic, as is the exchange at the end of the book when the travellers stand 'halfway across the world from Cambridge' and quote Coleridge on the site of what was once the palace of Kublai Khan:

> Below, beside the Jeep, the Mongols stood shaking their heads. As we walked back towards them, the Party cadre revolved his index finger in his temple. He grunted something in Mongol. Then he translated it for us. 'Bonkers', he said. 'English people very, very bonkers.' 'Personally', said Louisa, as we got back into the Jeep, 'I think he could well have a point'. (Dalrymple, 1990)

The convention of travel writing invites us to accept conversations of this kind as factual, not as fictitious. And we are constantly in a position of uncertainty about language: can our travellers really be such superb linguists that they can converse with anyone and everyone as they cross continents? Or do they continually and fortuitously meet local people whose English is not only fluent, but good enough for jokes and insider references? These conversations are presented as factual and authentic. If they are meant to have actually taken place, then the quality of authenticity is conveyed by their seemingly being translations. On the other hand, the fact that they appear to be translated dialogues may simply serve to blur the lines and make it impossible for anyone to deduce whether an original conversation ever took place at all. Readers are asked to believe in the veracity of the travellers tales, but the question of linguistic competence is thus carefully obscured. We collude with the idea that travellers can talk to anyone, anywhere in the world and record their conversations in the form of direct speech.

Fictitious Translation

The convention of the supposed translation is employed by travel writers to confer authenticity onto their accounts. Another convention, used occasionally by travel writers but more frequently by writers of fiction is the use of signs in the text to signal that a dialogue is taking place in another language. In particular, a convention that developed in the nineteenth century is the use of a mock medieval English that becomes a means of indicating that the speakers are not using English at all.

The device of mock medieval English to signal that the conversation was taking place in another language was a favourite of the authors of imperialist fiction such as Rider Haggard. Haggard's *Allan Quatermaine* (1887) contains particularly good examples. In this novel, Quatermaine, the narrator, who is an old man trying to come to terms with the death of his son, goes to Africa with his trusted companions, Sir Henry Curtis, Captain

John Good, and the Zulu warrior Umslopogaas. After a series of harrowing adventures, the travellers reach an unknown kingdom, ruled by two queens, Nyleptha, the blonde, blue-eyed good queen, and Sorais, the dark-haired bad one. They arrive in a boat, and their first act is to shoot some of the hippos in the shallow waters beside the great city. This makes them guilty of sacrilege, since the hippos are sacred, and they are then the object of the intense hatred of the high priest, Agon who wants them destroyed. Both queens fall in love with Sir Henry, who only returns Nyleptha's affections. Sorais and Agon plot to kill the intruders, but the plan fails and finally Sir Henry and Nyleptha agree to marry. The moment when this decision is taken offers a clear example of the use of implied translation in the text. Agon has been defeated, and a decision has to be taken about what to do with him:

> 'Well', said Sir Henry, 'if we are to imprison him, I suppose that we may as well let him go. He is of no use here'. Nyleptha looked at him in a curious sort of way, and said in a dry little voice. 'Thinkest thou so, my lord?' 'Eh?' said Curtis. 'No, I do not see what is the use of keeping him'. She said nothing but continued looking at him in a way that was as shy as it was sweet. Then at last he understood. 'Forgive me, Nyleptha', he said, rather tremulously. 'Dost thou mean that thou wilt marry me even now?' 'Nay, I know not, let my lord say', was her rapid answer, 'but if my lord wills, the priest is there and the altar is there' — pointing to the entrance of a private chapel — 'and am I not ready to do the will of my lord?' (Haggard, 1887)

The use of this pseudo-medieval language is meant to signal that this is a translation, from the Zu-Vendi, the language they are supposedly speaking. Nyleptha uses this language throughout, but Sir Henry shifts from blunt plain English to mock medieval, indicating that he has moved into Zu-Vendi. Moreover, the novel shows very clearly that plain English is by far the most desirable language. When the couple marry, Quatermaine notes that Nyleptha listens attentively to Agon's words, concerned 'lest Agon should play her a trick, and by going through the invocations backwards divorce instead of marry them'. Once the Zu-Vendi ceremony is over, Quatermaine offers to read the English marriage service, an offer taken up promptly by the bridegroom who points out that he does not feel 'half married yet'.

Language in this novel is highly significant. English is the language of honesty, decency and nobility. Zu-Vendi is foreign, and that foreignness (and hence inauthenticity, duplicity and vagueness) is signalled by the mock medievalising. The fake medieval, like the fake pidgin English, is a textual strategy that is full of meaning, for it implicitly downgrades both the speaker and the foreign language, implying that they are lower in status, intelligence and all kinds of other attributes than the Englishmen. That this strategy finds its way so quickly into travel writing deserves further attention and raises important questions about the transparency of the travel writer's representations of otherness through language.

Conclusions

What may be concluded from this short survey of problematic types of 'translation' is that the category of 'translation' is vague and unhelpful. This has been true for a long time, hence all the quibbling about determining the difference between 'adaptations' and 'versions' and 'imitations', all the arguing about degrees of faithfulness or unfaithfulness and the obsessive concern with the idea of an 'original'.

The medieval world had a far more open attitude to translation and writers do not seem to have operated with a binary opposition between translation and original, but with a cline along which the meaning of those terms passes through many different shades. Indeed, as has been so often demonstrated, the concept of the original is a product of Enlightenment thinking. It is a modern invention, belonging to a materialist age, and carries with it all kinds of commercial implications about translation, originality and textual ownership.

Mallory's *Morte d'Arthur* cannot be described as a translation, in one respect, because there is no explicit source text, but neither can it be described as an original because there is in fact a body of source material upon which Mallory's version is based. The author plays with this dichotomy, implying throughout that he is following an 'original' French author, but never clarifying who or what that original is.

The problems of defining what is or is not a translation are further complicated when we consider self-translation and texts that claim to be translated from a non-existent source. Becket's self-translation is not, under any stretch of the imagination or following any of the existing definitions of equivalence a translation. But it is clearly stated to be a translation, and consequently any reading has to take that into account. Burton's *Kasidah* claims to be a translation, indeed a scholarly translation, but it is not. Or is it? We may well speculate that he could not have written it at all if he had not known Arabic so well and tried so hard to write his own Arabic text in English. Burton was effectively inventing his own work as a translation.

The hugely popular genre of travel writing has translation at its heart. But what sort of translation? Are actual dialogues translated into English, or is broken English rendered into standard for reading facility? Or are totally fictitious dialogues presented implicitly as translations in order to establish the author's credibility? The question of authenticity is crucial here, for the veracity of the author is at stake. Inviting the reader to collude with the idea that a translation has taken place reinforces the writer's veracity.

That issue of veracity returns again when we consider dialogue in non-standard English in travel books or in fiction, that is dialogue presented as a translation though without ever stating that this is the case. Here the category of 'translation' is marked by the use of a particular type of language, and the notion of a translation serves to emphasise the good faith of the narrator, who apparently offers an unmediated text. Haggard goes much further and implies the superiority of English, contrasting the obviously fake medieval that signifies the foreign with the bluntness and honesty of everyday English. That the idea of translation can be used so blatantly for ideological manipulation is significant.

The starting point for this essay was a growing sense of discomfort with definitions of translation, and in particular with the moralising discourse of faithfulness and unfaithfulness. Gideon Toury helpfully introduces the concept of the pseudotranslation, but once we start to consider the way in which both the terminology of translation and the idea of an authentic 'original' that exists somewhere beyond the text in front of us are used by writers, then the question of when a translation is or is not taking place becomes increasingly difficult to answer. It is probably more helpful to think of translation not so much as a category in its own right, but rather as a set of textual practices with which the writer and reader collude. This suggests that literary studies, and discourse analysis in particular, need to look again at translation, for the investigation of translation as a set of textual practices has not received much attention. This is doubtless because we have been far too obsessed with binary oppositions within the translation model and have been too concerned with defining and redefining the relationship between translation and original. Even where the model of dominant original and subservient translation has been challenged, the idea of some kind of hegemonic original still remains — either in the source or target language. It is time to free ourselves from the constraints that the term 'translation' has placed upon us and recognise that we have immense problems in pinning down a term that continues to elude us. For whether we acknowledge it or not, we have been colluding with alternative notions of translation all our lives.

References

F.B. (1880) *The Kasidah of Hají Abdú El-Yezdí.* London: Bernard Quaritch.

Barthes, Roland (1977) The death of the author. Ed. and transl. Stephen Heath *Image, Music, Text* (pp. 142–149). London: Fontana.

Beckett, Samuel (1961) *Poems in English*. New York: Grove Press.

Borges, Jorge Luis (1964) Transl. James E. Irby 'Pierre Menard, author of the Quixote.' In Donald A. Yates and James E. Irby (eds) *Labyrinths* (pp. 62–72). Harmondsworth: Penguin.

Byron, Robert (1937) *The Road to Oxiana*. London: Macmillan.

Dalrymple, William (1990) *In Xanadu: A Quest*. London: Flamingo.

Derrida, Jacques (1985) 'Des Tours de Babel.' Transl. Joseph F. Graham. In Joseph F. Graham (ed.) *Difference and Translation*. Ithaca: Cornell University Press.

Godard, Barbara (1995) Theorizing feminist discourse/translation. In Susan Bassnett and André Lefevere (eds) *Translation, History and Culture* (pp. 87–97). London: Cassell (first pub. Pinter, 1990).

Rider Haggard, H. (1887) *Allan Quatermain*. London: Longmans, Green and Co.

Mallory, Thomas (1969) *Morte d'Arthur* (2 vols). Harmondsworth: Penguin.

McLynn, Frank (1990) *Burton: Snow Upon the Desert*. London: John Murray.

O'Hanlon, Redmond (1984) *Into the Heart of Borneo*. Edinburgh: The Salamander Press.

Sarup, Madan (1994) Home and identity. In George Robertson, Melinda Mash, Lisa Tickner, Jon Bird, Barry Curtis and Tim Putnam (eds) *Travellers' Tales: Narratives of Home and Displacement* (pp. 93–105). London: Routledge.

Toury, Gideon (1985) Translation, literary translation and pseudotranslation. *Comparative Criticism*, Vol. 6 (pp. 73–85). Cambridge: Cambridge University Press.

Venuti, Lawrence (1995) *The Translator's Invisibility*. London and New York: Routledge.

Chapter 3

Translation Practice(s) and the Circulation of Cultural Capital: Some Aeneids in English

ANDRÉ LEFEVERE

The object of the majority of translations that are produced in our day and age is the communication of information, be it about computers, cars, infusion pumps, and the like. The object of other translations — and they are a minority now, though they may not always have been — is the circulation of cultural capital. The difference between information and cultural capital, in the sense in which the latter term has been introduced by Pierre Bourdieu, could be succinctly formulated as follows: information is what you need to function on the professional level, whereas cultural capital is what you need to be seen to belong to the 'right circles' in the society in which you live.

The object of a third type of translations could be said to be situated on the level of entertainment: novels are translated, movies dubbed or subtitled, whereas the object of a fourth type of translations could be said to try to persuade the reader to adopt some course of action, as opposed to another. This rough distinction between four types of translation is predicated on the existence of, roughly, four types of texts. It is much too rudimentary, of course, not least because many texts that convey information or try to persuade also try to do so in a somewhat entertaining manner, whereas many texts that are primarily produced to provide entertainment can also be said to provide information and, at times, to succeed in persuading.

In what follows I am, however, concerned with the second type of texts/translations, namely those texts which, whether their primary aim may have been to provide information, entertainment, or a mixture of both, or to try to persuade, have become recognised as belonging to the 'cultural capital' of a given culture, or of 'world culture'. That cultural capital is transmitted, distributed, and regulated by means of translation, among other factors, not only between cultures, but also within one given culture. There have been attempts to transmit cultural capital on a grand scale in

41

the history of translation: the so-called 'translation schools' of Toledo and Baghdad come to mind, as does Mehmet Ali's policy of introducing French science, art, literature, and technology into Egypt at the end of the eighteenth and the beginning of the nineteenth century. I am not concerned with those attempts here. Rather, by pursuing the fortunes of some selected translations of Virgil's *Aeneid* into English — it is definitely not my intention to offer even an approximation of a 'history' of English translations of the *Aeneid* — I want to try to show how the concept of cultural capital can be made productive in the study of literary translation

Cultural capital, then, is the kind of capital intellectuals can still claim to have, and even, if only to some extent, to control, as opposed to economic capital, which most intellectuals do not even claim to have any more. Cultural capital is what makes you acceptable in your society at the end of the socialisation process known as education. Even if you are a nuclear physicist, or other highly specialised professional, you are expected to be able to participate in conversations on certain topics, ranging from Rembrandt to Philip Roth, from Watteau to Wittgenstein.

In the seventeenth century Virgil, and not only his *Aeneid*, was definitely considered to be cultural capital, indeed to be even at, or near, the very heart of the concept. That assumption is no longer as self-evident in our own time. David West (1990), a recent translator of the *Aeneid*, states somewhat defensively in his introduction that the text he has translated 'is not yet out of date' (viii). This statement is so lapidary that the very strength of the affirmation may well point to at least some subliminal doubts. Other modern translators take the course of analogy, linking aspects of the original to aspects of the times they live in. The aim is to convince readers that they are not wasting their time, that reading what they might consider 'old hat', but for the fact that it is still recognised as cultural capital, may well turn out to be a meaningful exercise after all. The strategy reveals itself as rather predictable. Robert Fitzgerald (1990), for instance, tells the reader he first read the *Aeneid* 'in the closing months of the Second World War', (414) and adds not only that 'our navy's Actium had been fought long before at Midway', (414) linking the decisive battles of the civil war between Antony and Augustus and the war in the Pacific, but also that 'the next landings would be on Honshu, and I would be there. More than literary interest' (414). Rolphe Humphries (1953) takes us to the McCarthy years, asking the rhetorical questions: 'What kind of propaganda is it to make the enemies, by and large, more interesting and sympathetic and colorful fellows than our own side?' (viii) and 'Shouldn't some patriotic organiza-tion investigate this subversive writer, secretly in the pay of a foreign power' (ix)? It remains for Allen Mandelbaum (1981) to bring in Vietnam:

'the years of my work on this translation have widened that personal discontent; this state (no longer, with the Vietnamese war, that innocuous word 'society') has wrought the unthinkable, the abominable' (xi). Bosnia, Ruanda, and ethnic cleansing will have to wait for the next translation, but there is no doubt in my mind that they will be found somewhere in the introduction to it.

The authors of the first English translations of the *Aeneid*, from Gavin Douglas to John Dryden and beyond, did not need to include such statements in their prefaces, nor would their audiences have expected them to do so, because to them Virgil was cultural capital, and of the highest order, though not just because he was Virgil. In John Guillory's formulation (1993), cultural capital is, first and foremost, '*linguistic* capital, the means by which one attains to a socially credentialed and therefore valued speech' (ix). In Dryden's time, Latin could still claim to be that speech; in Humphries' time this was definitely no longer the case. From Dryden to Singleton, therefore, translating Virgil also means giving your readers access to Latin, in one form or another, and it will become obvious that various forms were devised to do so. These various forms have one feature in common, though: they represent types of translations that do not try to replace their original, but to supplement it, whereas modern translations mainly try to replace it. Not knowing Virgil in Dryden's time might mean that one would be excluded from polite society, more specifically, and more importantly for the rising bourgeoisie, from the 'commerce', in all senses of the word, of that polite society. Not knowing Latin, on the other hand, would be sure to mean exclusion, barring access not necessarily to 'commerce' in the obvious sense of the word, but to the social mobility craved by those engaged in that kind of commerce, to 'the cultural and material rewards of the well-educated person' (ix).

In Dryden's time the aristocracy did not need upward mobility: it was either at the top, or it was beginning to slide down from that top, and it looked to economic, not cultural capital to arrest that slide. Cultural capital was sorely needed by the aspiring bourgeoisie, which would soon share its economic capital with the aristocracy in order to acquire that aristocracy's cultural capital. There was, in other words, no homogeneous audience for a translation of Virgil. Dryden realised this: in his introduction he complains that he was not able to devote as much time to his translation as he would have liked: 'that I wanted time is all I have to say; for some of my subscribers grew so clamorous that I could no longer defer the publication' (iii). Yet in the same introduction, which is dedicated to an aristocratic patron, Dryden quotes from Book X of the *Aeneid* in Latin, and goes on to say: 'I give not here my translation of these verses (tho' I think I have not ill succeeded in them,) because your Lordship is so great a master of the original that I have no reason to desire you should see Virgil and me so close together' (xxvii).

It is doubtful that all of Dryden's subscribers would have been as great 'masters of the original' as Dryden makes his Lordship out to be. Dryden, then, is translating for at least two audiences: the aristocratic one, which either does not need a translator to have access to the cultural capital represented by Virgil, or else upholds the pious fiction that it does not need one, and the bourgeoisie, especially the middle to lower bourgeoisie, which does need a translator and wants access not just to the text of Virgil, but also to Latin itself, and, in addition, also to the accepted discourse about Virgil's text. It is no coincidence, therefore, that Dryden's translation not only contains many notes of a more factual nature, but that he also engages in the discourse among Virgil's commentators, such as Macrobius, Pontanus, Ruaeus, and Segrais, whose 'principal objections' to Virgil he identifies in his introduction as being directed 'against his moral, the duration or length of time taken up in the action of the poem, and what they have to urge against the manners of his hero' (xvii). Virgil's moral (i.e. his willingness to support the policies initiated by Augustus, a topic still mentioned by Humphries in his introduction, as stated above) and Aeneas' manners might not have been such great riddles to the part of the audience that had not been formally taught the classics at some length; to even recognise the problem of the 'length of time' as a problem, on the other hand, that part of the audience would have to be told about the various theories of the epic current in Dryden's time, especially the French ones, which insisted that the action of the epic should not take longer than one year.

The distribution and regulation of cultural capital by means of translation, then, depends on at least the following three factors, to which more will be added as our analysis proceeds: (i) the need, or rather needs, of the audience, or rather audiences, a factor I shall address last, (ii) the patron or initiator of the translation, and (iii) the relative prestige of the source and target cultures and their languages.

Let us start with the third factor. Whether Dryden's particular Lordship was indeed able to compare Dryden's own version with the Latin original is immaterial. What is important, though, is that the possibility not only existed, but defined, to a very great extent, how the translation would be read by at least part of its target audience. It is almost inconceivable to us now that there were, indeed, readers, and there must have been a fair number of them, who read the translation not for the information is could impart, as is now routinely the case, but to see, quite literally, what the translator had done with, or to the text. Perhaps the closest analogy in our time is that of teachers of classics, who do not need the translations their students produce to understand the original, but who check those translations against the original to judge their students' understanding of it. This way of reading translations does, of course, put a greater onus on the translator: he (all the translators mentioned in this text turn out to be male) has obviously to measure himself against the original. Modern translators still claim to do so, and do, but not within a concept of translation predicated on the existence of a relatively great number of readers actually able to measure the extent to which the translator measures up against his author.

In the case of translations of the *Aeneid* published for about three hundred years after Gavin Douglas' translation was first published in 1553, Latin, and the Latin originals, was and were always there in the audience's and audiences' consciousness. Whether they were valued as part of a humanist education, or coveted as a tool for social advancement is, once again, immaterial. The fact remains that translations (not to mention original works) were produced in the shadow of Latin, not unlike the way English now casts its shadow on literary and cultural production all over the world.

To consider the second factor, patrons or initiators see to it that translations are commissioned, or at least put before the general public. It stands to reason, therefore, that they will have at least a say in shaping the strategies different translators select to produce their translations. In the case of Christopher Pitt's translation, the patron was none other than Pope himself. As John Conington (1900) writes in his history of the translation of the *Aeneid* into English, which is part of the long introduction to his own translation: 'Pitt was intimate with Spence, the friend of Pope; and the great poet, in words which seem not to have been preserved, signified his approval of an experiment which but for him would scarcely have been possible' (xxix). Two centuries later Cecil Day Lewis (1952) wrote for a totally different kind of patron: 'my own problem', he writes in his introduction, 'was simplified by the fact that the translation was commissioned for broadcasting' (viii). He then goes on to list the fundamental strategic decisions he made as a result: considerably more momentum would be required' (viii), 'variations of pace ... could be achieved better through verse' (viii), and 'the need to hold the listener's attention' (viii) led him to 'introduce here and there a sharp bold colloquialism or a deliberate cliché which might stimulate by appearing in an unfamiliar context' (viii). In most cases, though, patrons or initiators are less easily identifiable. They may simply be booksellers who detect a potential hole in the market, or even something as nebulous as 'the audience's expectations', which tend to become, at a given moment, very concretely embodied in the persons of the booksellers just mentioned. Conington has this to say about James Beresford's translation, which appeared in 1794: 'Cowper's "Homer" had recently appeared, and had been recognised to be, what it certainly is, a work of rare merit; and it was tempting to try whether the same process could not after all be made to answer with Virgil' (xxvii). That 'process' refers to the use of blank verse, rather than rhyme, as in Dryden's translation, and represents, therefore, a revision of Dryden's central position in the filiation of translations of the *Aeneid* into English.

G.K. Richards (1871) defined most succinctly what I am trying to convey by means of the term 'filiation', when he states that 'the version which the general judgment pronounces to be the best obtains possession of the field' (v). However, present day readers are likely to disagree with half of his estimate of what that version is. Richards singles out two translations 'which any new aspirant must regard as his most formidable competitors — viz. those of Dryden and of the late Professor Conington' (vii). Dryden still occupies that position to the present day, whereas Conington's translation did not survive him by many years. Yet even Dryden is no longer seen as a standard in terms of 'emulation' the way he once was: modern translators of the *Aeneid* still acknowledge Dryden's consummate craftsmanship, but they no longer feel called upon to actively challenge him. If anything, they tend to envy him. As Cecil Day Lewis observes: 'today we are in a less favourable position than Dryden was, for we have no style of our own in poetry, no artificial "literary" manner which could suggest the style of Virgil' (vii). If we think in terms of cultural capital, this is a further reason why fewer people are interested in reading Virgil nowadays. Not only do they not need access to Latin any more, but none of the current translations will, they feel, give them guaranteed access to a 'valorised' variety of English, not least because the very existence of any one such variety is, increasingly, subject to doubt.

Older translators approached Dryden in a different way. Christopher Pitt, who first published his translation in 1740, about forty years after Dryden first published his, feels the need to offer an 'apology' in his preface. 'To prevent the Reader's imagining', he writes, 'that I pretend to rival Mr. Dryden in his translation. There is no Name that I have a greater and more real Respect for' (vii). Pitt then goes on to confess: 'in different Places, I have borrowed about Fifty or Sixty entire lines from Mr. Dryden. I believe I need make no apology for the Liberty; but rather fear the Reader will wish I had borrowed a greater Number from his Noble Translation' (viii). One may well ask why Pitt then felt the need to produce a translation of his own. The answer lies not just in the challenge of emulation, because Pitt evidently thought that he would be fighting a losing battle against Dryden, let alone Virgil, but rather in the concept of patronage as referred to above: Pope wanted Pitt to try his hand at a translation. Once a certain translation has achieved a status that elevates it above all rivals, as Dryden's did, early on in the history of translations of the *Aeneid* into English, that translation can be seen, or at least thought, to influence subsequent translations in a negative manner, by making it all but unthinkable for subsequent translators to go beyond the parameters set by the translation that has become the standard. Dryden's use of rhyme, his opponents charge, has stifled innovation: 'the exigencies of rhyme form an immense impediment to that free choice of language which is needed to represent with the most exact propriety the sense of the translated author' (Richards xiii), and cursed translations with 'enervating diffuseness' (xv). The alternative to rhyme, blank verse, has not been tried often enough, Dryden's opponents believe, precisely because of Dryden's own success, even though blank verse 'is the metre of the English Epic, and therefore, in my opinion, the metre most fitted for reproducing the Epic of another nation' (Rhoades, 1893: viii).

To break the stranglehold the standard translation is thought to have, rival translators predictably resort to something like 'negative filiation', or the attempt to denigrate predecessors whose work may lay claim to the position of 'standard translation'. Gavin Douglas states that Caxton's retelling of the *Aeneid* is 'Ne na mair lyke' its original 'than the devill and Sanct Austyne' (8). Fairfax Taylor (1907) damns Dryden with faint praise: 'of the translations into modern English, that of Dryden may still be said to stand first, in spite of its lack of fidelity' (xii), and G.K. Richards tries to disqualify Conington as follows: 'the figure which rises behind the translator's page is not that of Publius Virgilius Maro, but of Sir Walter Scott' (xii) because, in Richards' opinion, of 'the tripping and jingling measure which is the fitting vehicle for Border legends or romaunts of chivalry' (x). In other words, Conington may have tried to increase the potential 'entertainment value' of his translation by taking over a way of writing narrative verse that had been made very popular by Sir Walter Scott. This, however, seems to have amounted to some kind of betrayal in the opinion of those who were of the view that potential entertainment value was not a factor to be seriously considered in the transmission of cultural capital.

In commenting on Conington's translation as he does, Richards illustrates another constant factor in the series we have been establishing, namely that of analogy. I have already briefly referred to it above on the level of what is usually called 'content' when discussing the attempts by modern translators of the *Aeneid* to convince their readers that the *Aeneid* is still worth reading, especially in translation. But analogy also exists on other levels. Fairfax Taylor hints at one of those levels when he writes: 'Virgil made use of the dactylic hexameter because it was the literary tradition of his day that epics should be written in that metre. In the same way it might be argued, the English tradition points to blank verse as the correct medium' (xiv). One compares both traditions — usually in a way that is somewhat prejudicial to one's own preference, and finds license in the original tradition for one's actions in the target tradition. Since both the original and the target traditions can, however, be interpreted in many different ways, it stands to reason that many different conclusions can be reached. Where Fairfax Taylor, for instance, invokes the tradition in support of blank verse as the ideal meter for a translation of Virgil, John Conington leans somewhat more in the direction of the target tradition and states that 'writing prose is now pretty well understood to be as much an art as writing verse' (xlviii). Accordingly, he translated the *Aeneid* in both verse and prose. David West interprets analogy in still another way and concludes: 'I know of nobody at the end of our century who reads long narrative poems in English, and I want the *Aeneid* to be read' (x).

Finally, analogy, or the lack of it, can also be seen to play a part on the level of ideology, the conceptual grid that consists of opinions and attitudes deemed acceptable in a certain society at a certain time, and through which readers and translators approach texts. Witness the sometimes heated discussions, lasting until about 1800, on how Aeneas treats Dido. After that the topic drops more or less from sight, but it is positively crying out to be revived and will no doubt enjoy a revival, with a vengeance, in the first feminist translation of the *Aeneid*. Translators before 1800 developed three basic lines of defence for Virgil, for Aeneas, or for both. Dryden blames it all on the gods: 'no less than an absolute command of Jupiter could excuse this insensibility of the hero' (xxxii), as Gavin Douglas had done before him: 'And gif that thir command maid him maynsworn,/That war repreif to their divinyte,/And no reproch onto the said Ene' (17). Pitt blames it all on Dido, calling her 'bold, passionate, ambitious, perfidious: but her most distinguishing characteristic is dissimulation' (9). Joseph Trapp (1735) blames Aeneas, but not Virgil: 'tho their [the gods] Impulse may in a great measure *excuse* him [Aeneas]; yet it does not *justify* him. It was a Fault therefore in *Him*, but not in the *Poet*'. (223).

Conversely, the Dido episode has also been used to reinforce the values of the target society, *ex negativo*. Gavin Douglas makes the moral point quite obviously in his introduction: 'Be the [Dido] command I lusty ladeis quhyte,/Be war with strangeris of onkouth natioun/Wyrk na syk woundris to their dampnatioun' (183). It is hard to imagine what else a bishop could have said on the subject, as soon as he resolved to say anything. Dryden, on the other hand, by no means a bishop himself, and writing in a society whose morals were not of the strictest, resorts to the following ironic comment: 'They [the ladies] may learn experience at her [Dido's] cost, and, for her sake, avoid a cave, as the worst shelter they can choose from a shower of rain, especially when they have a lover in their company' (xxxi).

Translators have to come to terms not just with different conceptual, but also with different generic grids. To do so, they must define themselves in terms of the poetics dominant in the target literature at the time the translation is made, and also in terms of the tension between the poetics of the source literature and that of the target literature — a tension that needs to be resolved by the translator. Most of the problems in this area are likely to be encountered in the domain of so-called 'form', rather than that of so-called 'content'. Dryden and his immediate successors took 'form' to extend to the very notion of the epic itself. Their thoughts on the subject also provide us with a clear example of filiation. Dryden praises Virgil's notion of the epic because it has 'nothing of a foreign nature' in it, 'like the trifling *novels* which Ariosto and others inserted in their poems' (ix), resolutely championing the classical concept of the epic against the 'romanzo' made popular by the work of not just Ariosto, but Boiardo as well. Pitt takes over Dryden's statement, with a literalism, even down to the italics, condoned by an earlier age, and amplifies it: 'nothing of a foreign nature, like the trifling novels, which Ariosto, and indeed Tasso and Voltaire inserted in their poems, by which the reader is misled into another sort of pleasure' (6). That pleasure subsequently turns out to be of the kind which 'softens and emasculates it [i.e. the soul] again, and unbends it to vice' (6). By including Tasso and Voltaire, as well as Ariosto, Pitt takes an even more uncompromising stand in defence of the classical epic, since Tasso's compromise, to blend the classical epic with the romanzo, had been all but accepted since the publication of both his own epic, the *Gerusalemme liberata*, and his theoretical work on the epic, the *Discorsi*. Finally, Trapp runs his own variation on Dryden's theme: :It is one thing to *describe* and *shew* the Passion (as *Virgil* does) ... and another thing to *describe* and *inflame* it (as *Ovid* does). But upon this Article few have more to answer for, than the Writers of Modern Romances and Novels' (193).

A century later, the early debate on the 'true' nature of the epic has been replaced by a debate on the choice between prose and verse, or two different types of verse in which to translate the *Aeneid*. Fairfax Taylor maintains that 'it seems clear that a prose translation can never really satisfy us, because it must always be wanting in the musical quality of continuous verse' (x). Perhaps the most pragmatic argument, in this context, was used by G.K. Richards to advertise the merits of his own translation. I quote it in full:

> The first six books of the *Aeneid* contain in the original 4755 lines.
> The version of Mr. Dryden 6495 lines.
> That of Mr. Pitt, in the same measure 6523 lines
> Mr. Conington's version contains, I believe, about 7300 lines.
> The adoption of blank verse has enabled me to include the whole in 5410 lines.

Obviously, the inflation, caused by rhyming couplets, that had started with Dryden and many others who, in James Rhoades' words 'have hampered themselves at starting with the exigencies of a rhyming metre' (viii), and had reached its runaway stage with Conington, needed to be stopped by the use of blank verse. If comparative length were, indeed, the only criterion for judging translations, Richards' translation would be better than those of the rivals he measures himself against.

Poetics also includes the use of diction, a diction that should, ideally, match both that of the original and that of the audience the translator is writing for. Dryden is fully aware of this, stating in his long preface not only that 'I am the first Englishman, perhaps, who made it his design to copy him [Virgil] in his numbers, his choice of words, and his placing them for the sweetness of sound' (li), but also that 'I have endeavor'd to make Virgil speak such English as he would himself have spoken, if he had been born in England, and in this present age' (lxi). Other translators have, predictably, been more reluctant to make Virgil speak the English of their time, and that English only, out of a sense of respect for Virgil's use of Latin, which includes words and phrases not exactly current in the Latin of his own time. Jackson Knight (1958), for instance, advocates a use of English that is occasionally 'slightly odd, for Virgil's Latin is liable to be odd' (22). At the same time he also calls for an English that should be 'as impersonal as possible, and not closely dated to the middle of the twentieth century' (22) though not, presumably, as impersonal and 'undated' as the language used in Victorian translations of the classics, which relied on a language they believed to be 'timeless' and which is now increasingly seen as merely archaic, and therefore counterproductive in terms of potential entertainment value, witness Fairfax Taylor's translation of the first lines of Book IV of the *Aeneid* as:

> Long since a prey to passion's torturing pains,
> The Queen was wasting with the secret flame,
> The cruel wound was feeding on her veins.

> Back to the fancy of the lovelorn dame
> Came the chief's valour and his country's fame (87)

Finally I will address the first factor, namely the need(s) of the potential audience(s). They are mainly responsible for the different strategies used by different translators at different times, indeed they can be seen to guide the translator's work on what is the most fundamental level, the level at which the most encompassing strategic decisions are taken. These different needs are, among other things, responsible for the existence, from the seventeenth century onwards, of a double lineage of Virgil translations into English: one, like Dryden's more concerned with emulating the original, without, however, neglecting to acquaint its reader at the same time with the current discourse about that original; and another, with many translators now forgotten, who tried to make the cultural capital represented by both Virgil and the language he wrote in, accessible to as many readers as possible, in as many forms as were believed to be helpful for that purpose. I shall now proceed to provide a brief discussion of these forms, and of the attitudes behind them.

In the introduction to his translation, first published in 1735, Joseph Trapp states that Virgil 'cannot be *relished* as a *Poet* unless he be in *Sense*, and *Construction, understood* as a *Writer*' (3). Trapp goes on to say that it is no less 'certain that there are, both in Town, and Country, many Gentlemen of fine Parts and Judgments, who have almost (tho' *not* quite) lost their Latin, or never understood *enough* to read *Virgil* in the original' (3). Those 'gentlemen' are the audience for Trapp's translation, and he consciously shapes that translation to respond to their needs, witness the following statement: 'the Notes being in English; the main Difficulty which these Gentlemen meet with in consulting Commentators is entirely removed' (Trapp 4). Trapp is referring here to the 'notes' often adapted from the canonised commentators referred to above. Unfortunately, these notes were written, and printed in Latin in most, if not all editions of the *Aeneid* available when Trapp published his own translation. The fact that the notes accompanying his translation were also in English will no doubt have counted as an additional 'selling point' for Trapp's work. At any rate, it allows him to state with great confidence: 'I am utterly mistaken if by the Help of this Version, and the Notes put together, they may not understand *Virgil* in *Latin*' (4).

There are also translations that attempt to straddle the fence. Some, like Andrews' translation, published in 1766, claim to be able to be both 'high literature' and a useful 'way into' the poem. Andrews states that his 'version is equally calculated' for 'such of our youth who are bred to learning', and adds, 'nor in the course of my work did I find these ends to be incompatible'

(8). His readers, who were warned to 'therefore expect more help in the grammatical construction' (8), may not have thought so, since his translation never went into a second edition. Andrews' stance toward the general diffusion of cultural capital is, significantly, by no means unambiguous. He laments the fact that 'the lesser degrees of it [i.e. learning] indeed, such as are immediately necessary to trade and commerce and to political caballing, seem like property to be more generally diffused among the commonality', adding that learning can, on the other hand, hardly boast 'of such eminent masters as in preceding centuries' (6–7). Andrews seems to suggest that those who are beginning to accumulate economic capital tend to take cultural capital for granted, and he is uneasy with that situation, displaying what is, in essence, an aristocratic reflex: because learning is more widely disseminated, it is no longer what it used to be.

It is interesting to note — and this point will be further illustrated in what follows — that the aristocratic reflex apparent in Andrews' preface, is entirely contradicted by Trapp's preface. For Trapp, the aspiring bourgeoisie should gain access to the classics by whatever means. Once the bourgeoisie is no longer 'aspiring', however, as soon as it occupies positions of real power, it begins to protect what has now become 'its' cultural capital against the kind of dissemination it regards as 'facile', as is apparent in Singleton's preface, referred to below.

Joseph Davidson is still on the side of the 'aspiring' bourgeoisie, trying to provide a useful 'way into' the *Aeneid* by trying to produce at least three books in one. His translation enjoyed a relatively high degree of popularity. It was first published in 1743, and reissued in 1801, 1810, 1813, 1821, 1830, 1831, 1848, and as late as 1906. Its title is worth quoting in full:

> *The Works of Virgil Translated into English Prose, as near the Original as the different Idioms of the Latin and English languages will allow with the Latin Text and Order of Construction on the same Page; and Critical, Historical, Geographical, and Classical Notes, in English, from the best Commentators both Ancient and Modern, beside a very great Number of Notes entirely New. For the Use of Schools, as well as Private Gentlemen.*

In his book, Davidson gives about three to five lines of the original text at the top of the page. Under it he gives his translation and his notes, as twentieth century readers would expect, but he also gives something else, which he even gives pride of place: under the original and above the translation and the notes. That something is called the 'ordo', the logical syntactic sequence of the words, taken out of their alignment in lines of verse and rewritten as prose. The technique is, of course, tributary to a long tradition of teaching Latin, in which the student was supposed to 'construe' the text, in order to better understand it. It is this 'grammatical construction' Andrews also writes about, as quoted above.

Let us turn to the first two lines of Book IV to make matters clearer. The Latin reads: 'At Regina, gravi iamdudum saucia cura,/Vulnus alit venis, et caeco carpitur igni'. This Davidson reproduces at the top of the page. Then follows the 'ordo': 'At Regina, iamdudum saucia gravi cura, alit vulnus *in suis* venis, et carpitur caeco igni *amoris*'. Davidson has done what generations of teachers of Latin have done before him: take the poetry out of the poetry so that its meaning, or rather, its sense, as Trapp called it, becomes more obvious. He has also added, in italics, words that are obviously not in the text of the *Aeneid*, but are to be supplied by the reader if the text is to make sense. Davidson spells them out to make sure that sense is properly understood. Whereas Virgil says: 'But the queen, already weighed down with heavy care, feeds the wound with her veins and is swept away by a blind fire', Davidson's ordo reads, in English: 'But the queen, already weighed down with heavy care, feeds the wound with her *very own* veins and is swept away by *the* blind fire *of love*'. Davidson's own translation reads: 'But, long before *his Speech was done*, the Queen, pierced with *Love's* painful Darts, feeds a Wound in every Vein, and consumes by slow Degrees in Flames unseen' (1). Again, Davidson has added italics to make sure the sense is properly understood. *His Speech was done* refers to the end of Book III, the previous book of the *Aeneid*, which closes with the end of Aeneas' story of the fall of Troy and his subsequent wanderings on the way to found a new city, as ordained by the gods. As she watches Aeneas tell the story and listens to his words, Dido falls in love with him. Book IV begins with the lines that make this obvious to the reader. The italicised '*Love*' needs no further explanation. Finally, Davidson adds the following note to his translation of the first two lines of Book IV: 'Love's painful Darts. This easy Metaphor in English seems best adapted to convey the force of the original *gravi cura, heavy* or *oppressive Care*; especially since Virgil uses the words *saucia* and *vulnus*, probably in allusion to the Darts and Arrows with which Cupid was poetically represented' (3). The present day reader might agree to the extent that 'Love's painful Darts' is an 'easy' metaphor, but for her or him that would precisely be a reason not to use it. Davidson obviously thought differently. This brings us to another important factor that comes into play when cultural capital enters the currency exchange, namely the poetics dominant in the target literature at the time the exchange is made, and somewhat beyond that time as well: there appears to be a time lag between the poetics that guide the production of original work and the production of translations.

Toward the middle of the nineteenth century, Conington sums up the situation as follows:

> [Bohn's Classical Library] is a proof that a considerable portion of the reading public, for different reasons, deserves to have the classics made accessible into English. Schoolboys are as fond of 'clandestine refuges' now as they were in Trapp's days; schoolmasters are, we fancy, beginning to tolerate, under certain modifications, what they cannot exterminate ... those who acquire the classical languages with little or no help from masters — probably an increasing class — find the book a natural substitute for the teacher; and there is a large class of readers to whom Latin and Greek are as unattainable as Coptic, yet who are interested in knowing what the ancients thought and said (xlviii).

The operative word for Conington is obviously still 'deserves'. He goes on to list different forms of 'accessibility': from the cribs schoolboys use, over the kind of book Davidson produced, to the Bohn Classical Library, which published his own translation. But the ground is shifting: whereas the first two groups Conington refers to are still given access to both Virgil and Latin, in some form, the last one no longer is. Conington's translation is one of the first to try to replace its original for a certain type of reader.

R.C. Singleton is among the last to take the opposite approach. To him translation, or rather, translations that are easy to read, as those in the Bohn Classical Library series were intended to be, though they did not always turn out that way, since many of them were written in what aspired to be 'timeless' Victorian English, is an abomination because it makes the cultural capital represented by the classics available to all and sundry, whether they work for that privilege or not. Here, according to Singleton, lies the profound iniquity that needs to be combated, in both economic and moral terms. Accordingly, Singleton proclaims in his introduction that 'translations of the whole of Virgil can readily be had for one-half of what the present volume will cost; while it contains no more than half of the whole work' (x). That 'present volume' has a title that reflects Singleton's project: *The Works of Virgil, Closely Rendered Into English Rhythm and Illustrated from British Poets of the 16th, 17th, and 18th Centuries*. That project has its own ineluctable logic. Since, Singleton posits, 'it will be found that a chief element of success' in instances of good writing, whether in Dickens or in *The Times*, 'lies in their rhythm' (viii), students have to learn to translate rhythmically. To help them in this task, 'it has been thought advantageous to give some extracts from the elder British poets, in the shape of notes' (xxiv). When Dido, for instance, reaffirms her vow not to marry again after her first husband's death, saying, in Singleton's translation: 'If rested not within my mind [resolve]/Firm and unshaken, not to wish to yoke/Myself to any in the marriage-bond' (133b), her words are underscored by the following extract from Beaumont and Fletcher's *The Knight of Malta*: 'She must not rest near me. My vow is graven/Her in my heart, irrevocably breathed/And when I break it —' (133). In the end, the student has no option but that of success, as long as he follows the course Singleton charts for him: 'the student, then, having once secured his words and phrases from the English poets, Virgil having supplied the ideas and the imagery, let him throw what he has acquired into rhythm' (xv). The truly remarkable aspect of Singleton's project is that he may well be among the last to try to walk an ever thinning red line between two types of 'socially credentialed' and 'valued' speech: Latin, which was losing its claim to that status, and a certain kind of English, precisely that of 'Dickens and *The Times*', which has all but taken it over. That is why translation, to him, should also be an exercise in composition, which will still not quite replace the original, but stands poised to do so.

In the meantime, though, Singleton is irked by the fact that those who struggle through twelve years of grammatical drudgery to earn finally the competence and the right to read Virgil, in the original, are cheated of the fruits of their labour by what he calls 'almost any translation' (see below), which makes Virgil available even to those who have not suffered for twelve years. Accordingly, Singleton delivers the following stern verdict: 'for I cannot but think it no trifling evil, when a young boy is possessed of a translation of an author which forms a part of his studies' (xi). Cutting corners is bad, and not only for young boys, but for all those who sustain 'serious moral injury' by availing themselves 'of aid which is usually forbidden' (xi). Instead, Singleton's translation is intended 'for the tutor's use' (xv). The tutor, one feels, is in the front line against philistine attacks, it is his duty to make sure that the classics are, and continue to be read in the original. To carry out his appointed task without straying from the straight and narrow, the tutor, therefore, needs all the help he can get, including Singleton's translation, for 'how often will weariness and want of spirit, headache and exhaustion, the consequences of mental exertion, lead the tutor to hail almost any translation as a boon! In such hours of debility perhaps the present may not prove unacceptable to him' (xvi). It is precisely to prevent the tutor from succumbing to 'almost any translation' that Singleton offers his own.

He had no way of knowing that this side of his project was fast sliding into the past, and that only a hundred years after his translation was first published, the precipitous decline of Latin in the educational system, which monitors the creation and circulation of cultural capital to a much greater extent than translation, had created a situation in which Conington's schoolmasters who 'tolerate ... what they cannot exterminate' have become the rule, rather than the exception, and that translations would, from now on, replace their originals, rather than supplementing them, giving their readers Virgil only, not Virgil and some access to Latin, without attempting, though, to teach them to write the new 'socially credentialed' and 'valued' speech.

References

Andrews, Robert (1766) *The Aeneid of Virgil*. London: Printed by Assignment from Robert Andrews.

Conington, John (1900) *The Works of Virgil*. Philadelphia: David McKay.

Davidson, Joseph (1801) *The Works of Virgil translated into English Prose, as near the Originals as the different Idioms of the Latin and English languages will allow with the Latin Text and Order of Construction on the same Page; and Critical, Historical, Geographical, and Classical Notes, in English, from the best Commentators both Ancient and Modern, beside a very great Number of Notes entirely New. For the Use of Schools, as well as Private Gentlemen*. London: Printed by Assignment from Joseph Davidson.

Day Lewis, Cecil (1952) *The Aeneid of Virgil*. London: The Hogarth Press.

Douglas, Gavin (1971) *The Aeneid of Virgil translated into Scottish Verse*. New York: AMS Press [Edinburgh 1839].

Dryden, John (1940) *Virgil: The Aeneid. Translated by John Dryden. With Mr. Dryden's Introduction*. New York: The Heritage Press.

Fairfax Taylor, E. (1907) *The Aeneid of Virgil*. London, Toronto, New York: Dent and Dutton.

Fitzgerald, Robert (1990) *The Aeneid. Virgil*. New York: Vintage Books.

Guillory, John (1993) *Cultural Capital*. Chicago and London: The University of Chicago Press.

Humphries, Rolfe (1953) *The Aeneid of Virgil*. London and New York: Scribner's.

Jackson Knight, W.F. (1958) *Virgil. The Aeneid*. Harmondsworth: Penguin Books.

Mandelbaum, Allen (1981) *The Aeneid of Virgil*. New York: Bantam Books.

Pitt, Christopher (1763) *The Works of Virgil in English Verse*. London: R.& J. Dodsley.

Rhoades, James (1893) *The Poems of Virgil*. Oxford: Oxford University Press.

Richards, G.K. (1871) *The Aeneid of Virgil*. Edinburgh and London: William Blackwood and Sons.

Singleton, R.C. (1855) *The Works of Virgil, Closely Rendered Into English Rhythm and Illustrated from British Poets of the 16th, 17th, and 18th Centuries*. London: Bell and Daldy.

Trapp, Joseph (1735) *The Works of Virgil translated into English Blank Verse with large Explanatory Notes and Critical Observations by Joseph Trapp, D.D.* London: Printed by Assignment from Joseph Trapp.

West, David (1990) *The Aeneid*. London: Penguin Books.

Chapter 4

Transplanting the Seed: Poetry and Translation

SUSAN BASSNETT

There are countless book-shelves, probably enough to fill entire libraries, of self-indulgent nonsense on poetry. In comparison with the quantity of poetry actually produced, the amount of redundant commentary must be at least double. A great deal of this literature claims that poetry is something apart, that the poet is possessed of some special essential quality that enables the creation of a superior type of text, the poem. And there is a great deal of nonsense written about poetry and translation too, of which probably the best known is Robert Frost's immensely silly remark that 'poetry is what gets lost in translation', which implies that poetry is some intangible, ineffable thing (a presence? a spirit?) which, although constructed *in* language cannot be transposed *across* languages.

A good deal of the fault lies with post-Romanticism, with its vague ideas about poets as beings set apart from other people, divinely inspired and often motivated by a death wish. A comedian on stage has only to fling a black cloak around himself for an audience to cry: Poet! and laugh. This image of the poet as an effete young man (women do not feature in this myth!) of delicate sensibility has further been encouraged in the Anglo-Saxon world by questions of class consciousness, for as English literature established itself in the universities in the early years of this century, so poetry rose up the social scale, away from the masses and towards an intellectual and social elite who took it over and claimed it as their own.

This sorry state of affairs, happily, is by no means universal. Poets have very different functions in different societies, and this is a factor that translators need to bear in mind. In former communist Eastern Europe, for example, poetry sold in big print-runs (now replaced by western soft-porn and blockbuster crime novels); poets were significant figures, who often spoke out against injustice and oppression. Likewise in Latin America, and in Chile, after Pablo Neruda's death in 1973 people took to the streets, and even illiterate peasants and workers in the barrios could quote from his vast poetic output.

Neruda saw the role of the poet as speaking for those who had no power to speak. The poet, for him, gave a voice to the voiceless. Elsewhere the poet has taken on the role of the conscience of a society, or as its historian. In some cultures, the poet is a shaman, a creator of magic, a healer. In others the poet is a singer of tales, an entertainer and a focal point in the community. If we consider how many times poets have been imprisoned, tortured, even killed, then we have some sense of the power that poets can hold. Queen Elizabeth I, herself a poet and translator, presided over the passing of laws that condemned to death those Irish bards whose role was seen as subversive and treasonable. This brief sketch of the diverse roles of the poet underlines the fact of the different function of poetry in different cultural contexts. This is of great significance for the translator, for such cultural differences may well affect the actual process of translating. Poetry as cultural capital cannot be consistently measured across all cultures equally.

Many writers have struggled to define the difficulties of translating poetry. Shelley famously declared that

> it were as wise to cast a violet into a crucible that you might discover the formal principle of its colour and odour, as to seek to transfuse from one language into another the creations of a poet. The plant must spring again from its seed, or it will bear no flower — and this is the burthen of the curse of Babel. (Shelley, 1820)

This passage is sometimes taken as an example of the impossibility of translation. It is as absurd to consider subjecting a flower to scientific analysis to determine the basis of its scent and colour as it is to try and render a poem written in one language into another. But there is another way to read Shelley's very graphic description of the difficulties of the translation process. The imagery that he uses refers to change and new growth. It is not an imagery of loss and decay. He argues that though a poem cannot be transfused from one language to another, it can nevertheless be transplanted. The seed can be placed in new soil, for a new plant to develop. The task of the translator must then be to determine and locate that seed and to set about its transplantation.

The Brazilian poet and translator, Augusto de Campos, one of the leading proponents of a post-colonial translation practice, rejects the notion that poetry belongs to a particular language or culture. 'A poesia, por definição, não tem patria. Ou melhor, tem una patria maior'. (Poetry by definition does not have a homeland. Or rather, it has a greater homeland) (De Campos, 1978). And if a text is not the property of any individual culture, then the translator has every right to help in its transfer across linguistic frontiers.

The history of translating and literary transfer would appear to bear out De Campos' proposition. How could we argue, for example, that Homer 'belongs' to Greece, since even contemporary Greeks have to learn the Greek in which he wrote as a foreign language. Equally, we might ask whether Shakespeare 'belongs' to England? Tolstoy, after all, declared that Shakespeare was primarily German:

> Until the end of the 18th century Shakespeare not only failed to gain any special fame in England, but was valued less than his contemporary dramatists: Ben Jonson, Fletcher, Beaumont and others. His fame originated in Germany, and thence was transferred to England. (Tolstoy, 1906)

The English, Tolstoy argues, failed to recognise the genius of one of their native writers and only learned about him in a roundabout way through the Germans. This is a disconcerting perspective if you are English, but serves to highlight the important role that is played so often by translation. For, as Walter Benjamin points out, translation secures the survival of a text, and it often continues to exist only because it has been translated (Benjamin, 1923).

The translation of Shakespeare across Europe in the late 18th and 19th centuries is a fascinating example of the intricacies of intercultural transfer and reinforces De Campos' point about textual homelands. For the writer who was so extensively translated into so many languages, at a point in time when great revolutionary ideals were sweeping across the continent, and concepts of national identity were being raised more forcefully than ever before was certainly not translated because of his specifically English origins. Shakespeare was not perceived as an emblem of Englishness, but was celebrated for his radical stagecraft, which challenged norms and expectations of good taste, and also for his politically charged subject matter. The Shakespeare who found his way into German, Russian, Polish, Italian, French or Czech was essentially seen as a political writer, whose texts raised crucial issues concerning power structures, the rights of the common people, definitions of good and bad government and the relationship of the individual to the state. A significant writer in the age of revolutions, we might say, though not everyone was of the same opinion. Voltaire, for example, was extremely critical:

> What is frightful is that this monster has support in France; and, at the height of calamity and horror, it was I who in the past first spoke of this Shakespeare; it was I who was the first to point out to Frenchmen the

few pearls which were to be found in this enormous dunghill. It never entered my mind that by doing so I would one day assist the effort to trample on the crowns of Racine and Corneille in order to wreathe the brow of this barbaric mountebank. (Voltaire, 1776)

Voltaire was complaining about the revolution in taste and effectively in dramatic poetics that writers such as Shakespeare provoked. And here, of course, we touch on a fundamental question in translation history which has special relevance to the translation of poetry: the impact upon a literary system that translation can have and the power of translated texts to change and innovate. But if poetry is indeed that which is lost in translation, how can such power be possible? The answer must surely lie in the ways in which translated texts have been received by the target system, and that in turn is inextricably linked to time, place and technique. For a translation to have an impact upon the target system, there has to be a gap in that system which reflects a particular need, and the skills of the translator have to be such that the end product is more than merely acceptable.

Frederic Will, a translator who has reflected at length upon the problems of translation, urges us to reconsider the relationship between the translation and the idea of an adamantine original:

Original texts are not icons. They are symbolically coded patterns of movement: intention, argument, and the expression of both, theme. They are neither hard nor soft, but are basically process. I like to think of them as participial, rather than nounlike or verblike. Works of literature, there to translate, have a character, a nature which is like their substance, their mark of personality; but they can make this substance clear, only by enacting it. That action is their verblike side, needed to reveal the nouns in them. In this sense they, literary originals, are participles. They enact the nouns they are by becoming verbs. They become verbs by enacting the nouns they are. (Will, 1993)

What Will is trying here to define is the special nature of a text, what he calls its 'mark of personality'. But he also reminds us helpfully that texts consist of language, they are composed of nouns and verbs and all kinds of lexical and grammatical patterns, and this is the dimension with which a translator needs to be primarily concerned. In order to translate poetry, the first stage is intelligent reading of the source text, a detailed process of decoding that takes into account both textual features and extratextual factors. If, instead of looking closely at a poem and reading it with care, we start to worry about translating the 'spirit' of something without any sense of how to define that spirit, we reach an impasse.

It is also often the case that the reading of a poem depends on the dialectic between the constituent elements of that poem on the page and extra-textual knowledge that we bring to it. One of my favourite contemporary poets is the Pakistani-British writer, Moniza Alvi. Her work derives from her experience as a woman belonging to more than one culture, and that hybridity is an essential part of her creativity. She writes from her own experience as a being in-between, a woman with a place in two cultures and consequently perhaps not entirely located in either. Her writing is therefore emblematic of the position occupied by millions in today's world. A theme to which she returns in many poems is that of belonging and not-belonging. One such poem is an eight line unrhymed work, *Arrival 1946* (Alvi, 1993).

The protagonist of the poem is a figure named only as Tariq who reflects on what he sees after he arrives at Liverpool and takes a train down to London. He looks out on 'an unbroken line of washing' and tries to square this with what he knows of the British:

> These are strange people, he thought –
> an Empire, and all this washing,
> the underwear, the Englishman's garden.

What Tariq does not know is that it is Monday, the traditional English washing-day. The fact of his not knowing this elementary fact about English life serves to accentuate his foreignness, and hints at difficulties to come. Moreover, the image of washing serves also to emphasise the contrast between what he sees in England and what he has seen of the superior British rulers In India, where presumably their washing was always kept out of sight and done by Indian servants. In this way, the contrast between the imperial ideal and the banal reality of daily life is underlined.

But it is not enough to know that Monday is washing day in order to understand what is going on in this poem. The image of washing reminds us of the old proverb about not washing dirty linen in public. Dirty linen, in this case is both actual and symbolic: the dirty linen of imperialism is symbolised by the linen that English people are hanging out to dry. And in Tariq's naive remark about the Englishman's garden, another set of references emerges. For the great poem of the imperial age, Kipling's *'The Glory of the Garden'*, presents all England as a garden, a magnificent garden surrounding a stately home, and kept in order by ranks of massed and willing gardeners. Concealed in the strata that make up this poem is the idealised English garden of the nineteenth century.

Any translator tackling this poem has a complex task indeed. The semantic items are straightforward, though the tight eight line format enables Alvi to foreground words at the start and end of lines. The last word of the poem is the adjective 'sharp', that has a large field of meaning. It is

used here to describe a Monday, and presumably refers to the state of the
weather, even as it hints at prospects of future pain. The principal problem,
though, is not lexical or grammatical or formal: it is the problem of the
knowledge required for a reader to be able to grasp the implications of the
text, most of which are only hinted at. The geographical data are precise. If
the reader does not know that Euston is a station in London, Tariq's journey
does not make much sense. The joke about washing provides the basic
structure of the narrative. Even the title is significant. Tariq has arrived in
England at a moment of in-betweenness. The Second World War ended in
1945, and the independence of India and creation of the state of Pakistan
was not to happen until 1947. Tariq is one of the first wave of immigrants
in the post-war period. He may be too early, or he may be too late. The
problems of how to transplant a poem like this, which has as its basis the
idea of cultural displacement and relies upon so much additional knowledge, test the translator both as reader and as writer.

James Holmes, a great translator of poetry across several languages and
distinguished scholar of translation, attempted to produce a basic set of
categories for verse translation. He lists a series of basic strategies used by
translators to render the formal properties of a poem. The first such strategy
he calls 'mimetic form', for in this case the translator reproduces the form
of the original in the target language. This can obviously only happen where
there are similar formal conventions already in existence, so that the
translator can use a form with which readers are already familiar. However,
Holmes points out that since a verse form cannot exist outside language, 'it
follows that no form can be "retained" by the translator' and no verse form
can ever be completely identical across literary systems (Holmes, 1970).
This means, therefore, that an illusion of formal sameness is maintained,
while in actuality the target language readers are being simultaneously
confronted with something that is both the same and different, i. e. that has
a quality of 'strangeness'. Holmes suggests that this is the case with
blank-verse translations of Shakespeare into German, and he argues that

> It follows that the mimetic form tends to come to the fore among
> translators in a period when genre concepts are weak, literary norms
> are being called into question and the target culture as a whole stands
> open to outside impulses. (Holmes, 1970)

The second strategy outlined by Holmes involves a formal shift.
Employing what he calls 'analogical form', he suggests that the translator
determines what the function of the original form is and then seeks an
equivalent in the target language. The most obvious example of this
technique would be the translation of the French alexandrine into English

blank verse and vice versa. Both these forms are employed in the classical drama of each of the two languages. Similarly, when E.V. Rieu produced his translation of Homer for Penguin in 1946, he argued in his preface that *The Iliad* should be seen as a tragedy and *The Odyssey* as a novel. Transforming his argument into practice, he then proceeded to render *The Odyssey* as a novel, in prose rather than in verse.

The third strategy is defined as 'content-derivative', or 'organic form'. In this process, the translator starts with the semantic material of the source text and allows it to shape itself. This is basically Ezra Pound's strategy when translating Chinese poetry, and has come to be a dominant strategy in the twentieth century, fuelled also by the development of free verse. In this kind of translation, the form is seen as distinct from the content, rather than as an integral whole.

Holmes' fourth category is described as 'deviant or extraneous form'. In this type of translation, the translator utilises a new form that is not signalled in any way in the source text, either in form or content. It might be possible to argue that Pound does this in parts of his *Cantos*, but on the whole it is more helpful to conflate Holmes' idea of the 'organic' and the 'extraneous' into a single strategy and use the term 'organic' for both. De Campos' translation of William Blake's '*The Sick Rose*' into a concrete poem, with the words in Portuguese shaped across a page to form petals of a flower, into the heart of which the text eventually disappears could be arguably 'organic' or 'extraneous' if we continue to use Holmes' terms. But such a distinction is pointless: what we can say is that De Campos' translation reflects a reading of Blake that demonstrates his sensitivity to the text and his desire to experiment in terms that would not have been accessible to Blake two centuries earlier.

Holmes suggests that the organic strategy has been most favoured in the twentieth century. However, it traces its ancestry clearly back to Shelley, whose use of organic imagery to describe the translation process has been referred to above. The idea of translation as an organic process is also clearly present in the thinking of Ezra Pound, who, like so many poets and translation theorists before and after was concerned to try and categorise what happens when a poem is rendered from one language into another.

Pound stresses the importance of the target language for translators. Discussing medieval poetry, for example, he remarks

> The devil of translating medieval poetry into English is that it is very hard to decide HOW you are to render work done with one set of criteria into a language NOW subject to different criteria. Translate the church of St. Hilaire of Poitiers into barocco? You can't, as anyone

knows, translate it into English of the period. The Plantagenet Kings'
Provençal was Langue d'Oc. (Pound, 1934)

Pound is being ironic here, for as he and everyone knew, a great deal of
medieval poetry had indeed been translated in the nineteenth century into
a mock medieval English, a kind of translationese that was intended to
signal a quality of antiquity about the source text. Pound's point is that this
is absurd: the end product is unreadable, because it is written in a language
that has no vitality, because it is completely fictitious.

Pound was concerned primarily with the translation of texts from earlier
periods or from non-Western cultures, hence his emphasis is less on the
problems of translating formal properties of verse, for he recognised that
forms are by no means equivalent across literatures. What he insists upon,
though, is that the translator should first and foremost be a reader. Through
his many notes and comments on translation, there is a consistent line of
thought, which attributes to the translator a dual responsibility. The
translator needs to read well, to be aware of what the source text is, to
understand both its formal properties and its literary dynamic as well as its
status in the source system, and then has to take into account the role that
text may have in the target system. Time and again Pound reminds us that
a translation should be a work of art in its own right, for anything less is
pointless.

He also makes another kind of distinction in his thinking about the
translation of poetry and endeavours to define elements that are more or
less translatable. There are, he suggests, three kinds of poetry that may be
found in any literature. The first of these, is *melopoeia* where words are
surcharged with musical property that directs the shape of the meaning.
This musical quality can be appreciated by 'the foreigner with the sensitive
ear', but cannot be translated, 'except perhaps by divine accident or even
half a line at a time' (Pound, 1928).

The second, *phanopoeia*, he regards as the easiest to translate, for this
involves the creation of images in language. The image was, of course,
central to Pound's poetics, as his deliberate choice of the highly imagistic
Japanese and Chinese verse forms as models demonstrates.

His third category, *logopoeia*, 'the dance of the intellect among words' is
deemed to be untranslatable, though it may be paraphrased. However,
Pound suggests that the way to proceed is to determine the author's state
of mind and start from there. We have come back again to Shelley and to
the notion of transplanting the seed.

Time and again, translation scholars struggle with the problem of the
inter-relationship between the formal structure of the poem, its function in
the source language context and the possibilities offered by the target

language. Robert Bly talks about eight stages of translation, (Bly, 1984). André Lefevere in his book on translating the poetry of Catullus talks about seven strategies and a blueprint (Lefevere, 1975) The missing element in so much writing about poetry and translation is the idea of the ludic, of *jouissance*, or playfulness. For the pleasure of poetry is that it can be seen as both an intellectual and an emotional exercise for writer and reader alike. The poem, like the sacred text, is open to a great range of interpretative readings that involve a sense of play. If a translator treats a text as a fixed, solid object that has to be systematically decoded in the 'correct' manner, that sense of play is lost.

A sign that informs us to 'Keep off the grass' is issuing an instruction. It is a four word text with a precise function, and if we were to translate it, we would be translating its functionality, not necessarily its semantic components. But what do we do with a four word text that is included in the works of the great Italian poet, Giuseppe Ungaretti:

M'illumino
d'immenso

We could start by taking a dictionary, and discovering that the first line consists of a reflexive verb, *illuminarsi* that can be rendered in English as 'to illuminate oneself/to light up oneself/to enlighten oneself'. The second line consists of the preposition *'di'* meaning 'of/with/from' and an adjective, *'immenso'*, meaning 'immense/huge/boundless', which is curious because we might expect the noun *immensita* here instead. So a rough version might be 'I am illuminated with the immense'. Or, 'I am immensely illuminated', or 'I am enlightened by immensity'. We should pause here, because it is becoming obvious that this four line poem, hailed as a great work in Italian, is dreadful in English. The translations veer between the banal and the pretentious. This would seem to be a classic case of Pound's logopoeia, of a text that is so embedded in the literary and philosophical traditions of its writer that it is not accessible to readers from another culture, despite apparent lack of semantic difficulties. To an Italian reader, the idea of *illuminare* and of *l'immensità* trigger whole fields of referents. These words are embedded into the cultural system. They cannot be translated literally, even though literal meanings exist. The only way for a translator to approach a text like this is to follow Shelley's organic principles, and endeavour to understand and absorb the text to such a degree within one's own system that a new plant can begin to grow. Yves Bonnefoy echoes this, when he says that we should try to see what motivates the poem in the first place, 'to relive the act which both gave rise to it and remains enmeshed in it' (Bonnefoy, 1989).

In his lucid essay on translating poetry, Octavio Paz makes a vital distinction between the task of the poet and the task of the translator:

> The poet, immersed in the movement of language, in constant verbal preoccupation, chooses a few words — or is chosen by them. As he combines them, he constructs his poem: a verbal object made of irreplaceable and immovable characters. The translator's starting point is not the language in movement that provides the poet's raw material, but the fixed language of the poem. A language congealed, yet living. His procedure is the inverse of the poet's: he is not constructing an unalterable text from mobile characters; instead he is dismantling the elements of the text, freeing the signs into circulation, then returning them to language. (Paz, 1971)

The poet plays with language and comes to create a poem by fixing language in such a way that it cannot be altered. But the translator has a completely different task, that involves a different kind of play. The translator starts with the language that the poet has fixed, and then has to set about dismantling it and reassembling the parts in another language altogether. Paz argues that this process of freeing the signs into circulation parallels the original creative process invertedly. The task of the translator is to compose an analogous text in another language, and the translator is therefore not firstly a writer and then a reader, but firstly a reader who becomes a writer. What happens, says Paz, is that the original poem comes to exist inside another poem: 'less a copy than a transmutation'.

This is a very helpful way of looking at the translation process, a very liberating way. It is, in terms of theory, related to Walter Benjamin's idea of the translation providing the life-hereafter of a text, enabling it to survive and sometimes even resurrecting it. It is a liberationist view of translating, because it never enters into the vexed question of whether a translation is or is not an inferior copy of an original. The task of the translator is simply a different kind of writerly task, and it follows on from the primary task of reading.

A translator to whom I have returned frequently over the years is Sir Thomas Wyatt, one of the poets credited with introducing the sonnet into English in the early sixteenth century. I keep coming back to Wyatt, because although he never formulated any views on translation, or at least if he did none have come down to us, his translation practice stands out even in an age of extensive translation activity. R.A Rebholtz, who edited the complete edition of Wyatt's poetry in 1978, was uncomfortable with Wyatt's translations, describing them variously as translations of Petrarch, free imitations and even very free imitations (Rebholz, 1978). His discomfort probably arises from the fact that if we set Wyatt's translations of Petrarch

alongside the originals, we come face to face with an example of Paz'
liberationist translation practice. Wyatt takes Petrarch as his starting point
and frees the signs into circulation for a completely different readership, in
another language and another age.

Petrarch's 'Una candida cerva sopra l'erba' (Rime 190) in Wyatt's version
becomes a completely new poem, with a different focus and altered tone.
The Italian text reads as follows:

Una candida cerva sopra l'erba
verde m'apparve, con duo corna d'oro,
fra due riviere, all'ombra d'un alloro,
levando'l sole, a la stagione acerba.
Era sua vista sì dolce superba,
ch'i lasciai per seguirla ogni lavoro,
come l'avaro, ch'n cercar tesoro,
con diletto l'affanno disacerba.
'Nessun mi tocchi – al bel collo d'intorno
scritto avea di diamanti e di topazi –
libera farmi al mio cesare parve'.
Et era 'l sol gia volto al mezzo giorno;
gli occhi miei stanchi di mirar non sazi,
quand'io caddi ne l'acqua, et ella sparve.

This is a poem full of classic Petrarchan imagery. It is structured in terms
of two basic units, 8 lines with an ABBA rhyme pattern that repeats, and
six lines with a repeating CDE pattern. There is a reference to his beloved
Laura, through the image of the laurel tree (*alloro*) and the setting of the
poem is the landscape of the courtly love-lyric: green meadows in
springtime, running water, early morning that gradually moves into
mid-day, a metaphor for the passing of a life time. The lover is represented
as passive — the white deer appears *to* him, he leaves everything he has
been doing to gaze upon her, he is still gazing enraptured when he falls into
the water and she vanishes.

Two elements are distinctive to this poem, however: the image in lines
7–8 of the miser, who enjoys collecting treasure so much that he ceases to
be aware of the effort it costs him, and the details in lines 9–11 of the collar
round the deer's neck. 'Let no one touch me', reads the message in
diamonds and topaz, 'it is for my Caesar to set me free'.

Wyatt's version is a transplanting of Petrarch's:

Who so list to hounte I know where is an hynde;
But as for me, helas, I may no more:
The vayne travaill hath weried me so sore,

I am of them that farthest cometh behinde;
Yet may I by no meanes my weried mynde
Drawe from the Diere: but as she fleeth afore
Faynting I folowe; I leve of therefore,
Sithens in a nett I seke to hold the wynde.
Who list her hount I put him out of dowte,
As well as I may spend his tyme in vain:
And graven with Diamonds in letters plain
There is written her faier neck rounde abowte:
'Noli me tangere for Caesar's I ame,
And wylde for to hold though I seme tame'.

There are several striking differences between the two poems. Firstly, and most obviously, Wyatt has altered the form of the sonnet to a rhyme scheme that runs ABBA ABBA, CDDC, EE. This has the effect of breaking the sonnet into three parts rather than two: there is an eight line unit, followed by a distinctive four line unit and then the poem culminates in the final couplet. This is the form that would later be taken up by Sidney, Spenser and Shakespeare, because what the final couplet offers a writer is a tremendous potential for ironic reversal, Whereas the Petrarchan sonnet is a more graceful, more integrated form in which the component parts of the rhyme scheme hold together more concisely, the English version foregrounds the last two lines and gives them infinite possibility. The sonnet, once a vehicle for courtly pronouncements of love or mystical expressions of the poet's relationship with the divine, has had its function extended, by the simple device of altering the pattern of foregrounding constructed by the rhyme scheme.

Wyatt makes other changes too. English, unlike Italian, demands the use of a pronoun with a verb, but even allowing for this grammatical factor, Wyatt's poem is full of self-referential 'I's and 'me's. The capitalising of the 'I' in English, as Southey famously noted, tends to stress the importance of the speaking subject. In a short poem such as this, the 'I' is foregrounded almost to excess. Where Petrarch's sonnet opens with a vision of the white deer that appears to the speaker, Wyatt's opens with a blunt piece of man to man advice to fellow huntsmen. Petrarch's deer may or may not be visionary; Wyatt's is made of flesh and blood. His pursuit of the deer has exhausted him, and the speaker complains about the effort that he has wasted in the attempt. The tone of the Petrarch sonnet is one of tranquillity, but the tone of the Wyatt poem is one of agitation and even anger.

The image of the miser cherishing his hoard is not present in the English, but significantly there is an image in exactly the same position, in lines 9–10.

Wyatt's image continues the motif of tiredness and frustration, through the
idea of a man trying to catch the wind in a net.

The most significant shifts occur in the last six lines. Wyatt's deer is
wearing a jewelled collar too, but its message is different. Petrarch's deer is
said to belong to Caesar who has the power to grant her freedom. There is
no reference to freedom in Wyatt's poem, and his deer wears a collar with
a Latin inscription and a warning about her savagery despite her apparent
docility.

We can begin to understand what has happened in the translation
process when we consider the contexts within which these two writers
created their very similar, yet very different texts. Petrarch's poem was part
of his sequence of poems that deals with his unrequited love for Laura and
his endeavours, through that love, to become closer to God. His use of the
term Caesar recalls the Biblical reference to the division of the earthly and
heavenly kingdoms. But Wyatt lived in another age, the age of Renaissance
Humanism, of Machiavelli and the new courts, the age when men began to
challenge not so much the existence of God but the idea of their abjectness
before God. The speaker in Wyatt's poem is not having a mystical vision of
any kind, he is engaged in the fruitless pursuit of a woman who belongs to
someone else and who appears to have been leading him on. His is the voice
of a cynical, disconsolate lover, who is giving up the chase in despair. That
this poem is _a clef_, and actually refers to Wyatt's love for Queen Ann Boleyn,
wife of Henry VIII in whose service Wyatt was employed, adds an
additional dimension to the reading.

Is Wyatt's poem a translation of Petrarch? Of course it is. It is a translation
that enables us to see how cleverly the translator has read and reworked
the source text to create something new and vital. He has kept the form of
the original, thereby introducing a new poetic form into the target system,
which bears out James Holmes' contention that mimetic form can indeed
have an innovatory function at key moments in literary history. However,
he has subtly altered that form, creating new possibilities for it in the target
language. He has maintained the image of the beloved as a white deer, but
has changed the relationship between the lady and the lover. The
perspective is different, and as a result the tone is different, though in
keeping with the age in which he lived and wrote. Paraphrasing Bonnefoy,
we can say that the energy generated by the source text has been sufficiently
great for the translator to follow it and in consequence create something
great of his own.

We may, at this juncture, make two assertions: firstly, that the translation
of poetry requires skill in reading every bit as much as skill in writing.
Secondly, that a poem is a text in which content and form are inseparable.

Because they are inseparable, it ill behoves any translator to try and argue that one or other is less significant. What a translator has to do is recognise his or her limitations and to work within those constraints. James Holmes suggests, helpfully, that every translator establishes a hierarchy of constituent elements during the reading process and then re-encodes those elements in a different ranking in the target language. If we compare translation and source, then the ranking of elements becomes visible. Holmes describes this process as a 'hierarchy of correspondences' (Holmes, 1978).

One of the most useful critical methods for approaching translation is the tried and trusted comparative one. When we compare different translations of the same poem, we can see the diversity of translation strategies used by translators, and locate those strategies in a cultural context, by examining the relationship between aesthetic norms in the target system and the texts produced. Crucially, the comparative method should not be used to place the translations in some kind of league table, rating x higher than y, but rather to understand what went on in the actual translation process.

Probably the most famous canto in Dante's *Inferno* is Canto V, when Dante meets the doomed lovers, Paolo and Francesca da Rimini in the second circle of hell, where the lustful are punished. The story of their illicit passion and of their murder by Francesca's husband, Paolo's brother, is related by Francesca herself, as she and Paolo are dragged past the horrified poet by an infernal black wind. The story of their love and brutal death so moves the poet, that he faints, an action that will have significance throughout his journey, since the fainting always coincides with moments when his own emotions overflow.

The high moment of Francesca's narrative is virtually a poem-within-a-poem:

> Amor, ch'al cor gentil ratto s'apprende,
> prese costui de la bella persona
> che mi fu tolta, e'l modo ancor m'offende.
> Amor, ch'a nullo amato amar perdona,
> mi prese del costui piacer sì forte
> che, come vedi, ancor non m'abbandona.
> Amor condusse noi ad una morte.
> Caina attende chi a vita ci spense'.
> Queste parole da lor ci fuor porte. (ll. 100–108)

Here Francesca summarises their story: she was overcome by love for 'la bella persona', whom she never names, and is still resentful of the manner of their death. The power of their love was so great that they are bound together in death for eternity, and their murderer will be allocated a place in the depths of hell after his death, that is yet to come.

For a thirteenth-century reader, one of the most obvious features of these lines is the direct reference to the famous poem by Guido Guinizelli, one of the founding members of the *dolce stil nuovo*, 'Al cor gentil rempara sempre amore'. Dante greatly admired Guinizelli, but here the implications are clear: illicit love leads downwards to hell, and Paolo and Francesca admit that their passion was kindled by reading a book of love poetry together. Through the deliberate references to the love poetry that he so admired and sought to produce himself, Dante is making a serious point about the need to put morality above aesthetics. Not only do readers have a moral responsibility, so also do writers. Dante as writer is therefore implicated in the downfall of these two lovers, and his pain on hearing their story is exacerbated by this awareness. A thirteenth-century reader would have had no problem understanding the point that is being made through the conscious references to the *dolce stil nuovo*. The anaphora of *amor* at the start of each three line unit signals the importance of the formal structure of this passage, making it stand out from the rest of the canto.

Translators have wrestled in various ways with these lines. Of the dozens of English translations, I have selected a sample, starting with Cary, author of the first complete translation of the *Divine Comedy*, through to Robert Durling (1996) whose new version of the *Inferno* has recently appeared. Cary (1814), who does not use rhyme, adopts a pseudo-medieval English, in keeping with early nineteenth century convention. Longfellow's 1867 version does likewise. Interestingly, Byron chose to translate Francesca's narrative, taking it out of the context of the rest of the canto. Charles Eliot Norton, in 1941, turns the whole work into prose, but keeps the medievalised language. Dorothy Sayers' Penguin translation of 1949 is also written in mock medieval English, but she does use rhyme throughout. More recently, Sisson (1980) and Durling (1996) have produced unrhymed versions in modern English.

Let us consider these different versions of the first six lines of this passage:

> Love, that in gentle heart is quickly learnt
> Entangled him by that fair form, from me
> Ta'en in such cruel sort, as grieves me still:
> Love, that denial takes from none beloved,
> Caught me with pleasing him so passing well,
> That, as thou seest, he yet deserts me not. (Cary: 1816)

Love, which the gentle heart soon apprehends,
Seized him for the fair person which was ta'en
From me, and even yet the mode offends.
Love, who to none beloved to love again
Remits, seized me with wish to please so strong.
That, as thou seest, yet, yet it doth remain. (Byron: 1820)

Love, that on gentle heart doth swiftly seize,
Seized this man for the person beautiful
That was ta'en from me, and still the mode offends me.
Love, that exempts no one beloved from loving,
Seized me with pleasure of this man so strongly,
That, as thou seest, it doth not yet desert me. (Longfellow: 1867)

Love, which quickly lays hold on gentle heart, seized
this one for the fair person that was taken from me, and the
mode still hurts me. Love, which absolves no loved one
from loving, seized me for the pleasing of him so strongly
that, as thou seest, it does not even now abandon me.
(Norton, 1941)

Love, that so soon takes hold in the gentle breast,
Took this lad with the lovely body they tore
From me; the way of it leaves me stil distrest.
Love, that to no loved heart remits love's score,
Took me with such great joy of him, that see!
It holds me yet and never shall leave me more. (Sayers, 1949)

Love, which quickly fastens on gentle hearts,
Seized that wretch, and it was for the personal beauty
Which was taken from me; how it happened still offends me.
Love, which allows no one who is loved to escape,
Seized me so strongly with my pleasure in him.
That, as you see, it does not leave me now. (Sisson, 1980)

Love, which is swiftly kindled in the noble heart,
seized this one for the lovely person that was taken
from me; and the manner still injures me.
Love, which pardons no one loved from loving in
return, seized me for his beauty so strongly that, as
you see, it still does not abandon me. (Durling, 1996)

All the translators, regardless of the form they have employed, maintain
the anaphora. But beyond this, what is most apparent are the differences

between the versions, and the incomprehensibility of parts of most of them. What happens in the Italian is that Francesca's narrative changes focus several times: she begins with a statement about love and the 'cor gentil', moves to describe how love overcame Paolo, then immediately shifts back to her own feelings, in the here and now. She is, she tells Dante, unable to forget the circumstances of her death, and this signals to the reader that she has not repented and is therefore justifiably condemned to hell. The foregrounding of 'm'offende' at the end of line 3, contrasts with 'perdona' at the end of line 4. Francesca is here, not because her husband did not pardon her, but because she has not been able to pardon him. The second three line unit opens again with a statement about love, though this time the negative emphasises love's cruel tyranny, then moves to describe the unending power of love over her. Her desire for Paolo endures even after death, though Cary offers a version of the line that makes Paolo, rather than 'piacer' the subject.

Space does not permit detailed examination of these translations, but if we return to Paz' image of the translator liberating the fixed signs set down by the original writer, and connect that to Shelley and Pound insisting upon the importance of the reading process that precedes the rewriting, then it becomes apparent that all the translators are in their different ways unable to break free of their source and appear uncertain about their readers. The prose versions are, if anything, the most obscure. Norton, Sisson and Durling all endeavour to simplify Dante and clarify the ambiguities in his writing, but their syntax, which reflects an attempt to follow the Italian, renders the meaning unclear. Longfellow is obsessed with the verb 'to seize', Byron appears to have put all his energy into lines 1 and 4 and left the rest to chance, Sayers uses colloquial language, turning the idealised medieval lover into 'the lad with the lovely body'. The translators appear caught between producing a close rendering of the source text and explicating that source for their readers. There is no sense of playfulness in any of them.

The problem they share here, of course, is that these lines are deliberately written in a particular style and are consciously ambiguous in their structure. It is not only the character of Francesca that emerges from these lines, it is also an autobiographically framed moral statement about the role of the writer. This aspect of the text has disappeared. In the nineteenth and twentieth centuries, the courtly love ideal and the medieval notion of sin and repentance have ceased to have meaning, except as intellectual curiosities. Dante's poem has become just such an intellectual curiosity itself. Editors and translators supply readers with detailed footnotes to enable them to access the text. The status of the work demands that it should be read and translated; Pound would argue that somewhere along the way, the idea of the *Divine Comedy* as a poem has evaporated.

Bonnefoy suggests that a work has to be compelling, or it is not translatable. Pound would certainly have agreed with this. For if translation is, as Lefevere and others claim, rewriting, then the relationship between writer and rewriter has to be established as productive. Translations of poems are part of a process of reading continuity. Writers create for readers, and the power of the reader to remake the text is fundamental. Different readers will produce different readings, different translators will always produce different translations. What matters in the translation of poetry is that the translator should be so drawn into the poem that he or she then seeks to transpose it creatively, through the pleasure generated by the reading. If we follow Bonnefoy's view, he would point out that none of the translators of Dante appear to have relived the act that gave rise to it and remains enmeshed in it; rather, they appear to have taken the source as a monolithic whole and chipped away at it. Justifying his own approach to translation, Bonnefoy talks about releasing a creative energy that can then be utilised by the translator.

The positive imagery of translation as energy-releasing, as freeing the linguistic sign into circulation, as transplanting, as reflowering in an enabling language is a long way removed from the negativity of Frost and the pundits of untranslatability. A great deal of this imagery has been around a long time, but it is only recently, as post-modernists reject the idea of the monolithic text, that a discourse of translation as liberating has come to the fore. The boundaries between source and target texts, never clearly determined in any genre, cannot be sustained if a poem is to have an existence as a poem in another language. Perhaps the most succinct comment on the symbiosis between writer and translator/rewriter of a poem are these lines by the Earl of Roscommon, Dillon Wentworth, composed more than three hundred years ago:

Then seek a Poet who your way does bend,
And choose an Author as you choose a Friend:
United by this sympathetic Bond,
You grow familiar, intimate and fond;
Your Thoughts, your Words, your Styles, your Souls agree
No Longer his Interpreter, but he.

When the rewriter is perfectly fused with the source, a poem is translated. That this happens so frequently is a cause for celebration. Poetry is not what is lost in translation, it is rather what we gain through translation and translators.

References

Alvi, Moniza (1993) Arrival 1946. *The Country at My Shoulder*. Oxford: Oxford University Press.

Benjamin, Walter (1969) [1923] *Illuminations*. Transl. Harry Zohn. New York: Schocken.

Bly, Robert (1984) The eight stages of translation. In William Frawley (ed.) *Translation: Literary, Linguistic and Philosophical Perspectives*. Newark: University of Delaware Press.

Bonnefoy, Yves (1992) [1989] Translating poetry. Transl. John Alexander and Clive Wilmer. In Rainer Schulte and John Biguenet (eds) *Theories of Translation. An Anthology of Essays from Dryden to Derrida* (pp. 186–192). Chicago and London: University of Chicago Press.

Byron, Lord (1959) *The Poetical Works of Lord Byron*. London: Oxford University Press.

de Campos, Augusto (1978) *Verso, reverso e controverso*. San Paolo: Perspectiva.

Cary, H.F. (1814) *The Vision of Hell, Purgatory and Paradise of Dante Alighieri*. London: Frederick Warne.

Durling, Robert M. (1996) *The Divine Comedy of Dante Alighieri. Vol I. Inferno*. New York and Oxford: Oxford University Press.

Holmes, James (1978) Describing literary translations: Models and methods. In James Holmes, Jose Lambert and Raymond van den Broek (eds) *Literature and Translation* (pp. 69–83). Leuven: ACCO.

Holmes, James (1988) [1970] Forms of verse and the translation of verse form. In James Holmes (ed.) *Translated! Papers in Literary Translation and Translation Studies* (pp. 23–33). Amsterdam: Rodopi.

Lefevere, André (1975) *Translating Poetry: Seven Strategies and a Blueprint*. Assen/Amsterdam: Van Gorcum.

Lefevere, André (1992) *Translation, Rewriting and the Manipulation of Literary Fame*. London and New York: Routledge.

Longfellow, Henry Wadsworth (1867) *Dante's Inferno*. London: George Routledge.

Norton, Charles Eliot (1941) *The Divine Comedy of Dante Alighieri*. Boston/New York: Houghton Mifflin.

Paz, Octavio (1992) [1971] Translation: Literature and letters. Transl. Irene del Corral. In Rainer Schultze and John Biguenet (eds). *Theories of Translation. An Anthology of Essays from Dryden to Derrida* (pp. 152–62). Chicago and London: University of Chicago Press.

Pound, Ezra (1954) [1928] How to read. *New York Herald*. Reprinted in T.S. Eliot (ed.) *Literary Essays of Ezra Pound* (pp. 15–40). London: Faber and Faber.

Pound, Ezra (1954) Hell. *The Criterion*, April, 1934. Reprinted in T.S. Eliot (ed.) *Literary Essays of Ezra Pound* (pp. 201–213). London: Faber and Faber.

Sayers, Dorothy (1949) *The Divine Comedy. Vol. I. Hell*. Harmondsworth: Penguin.

Shelley, Percy Bysse (1965) [1820] The defence of poesy. In *Complete Works V* (pp. 109–43). London: Ernest Benn.

Sisson, C.M. (1980) *The Divine Comedy*. Manchester: Carcanet.

Tolstoy, Leo (1970) [1906] Shakespeare and the drama. In Oswald LeWinter (ed.) *Shakespeare in Europe* (pp. 214–74) Harmondsworth: Penguin.

Voltaire (1995) Letter to the Comte d'Argental, 1776. Cited in Romy Heylen *Translation, Poetics and the Stage. Six French Hamlets* (pp. 27–28). London and New York: Routledge.

Will, Frederic (1993) *Translation, Theory and Practice. Reassembling the Tower*. Lampeter: Edwin Mellon Press.

Wyatt, Sir Thomas (1978) *The Complete Poems*. Edited by R.A. Rebholtz. Harmondsworth: Penguin.

Chapter 5

The Gates of Analogy:
The Kalevala in English

ANDRÉ LEFEVERE

In what follows I shall try to demonstrate the power of analogy in the construction of texts, or even systems of texts. Analogy is, I submit, the most potent factor in the process of acculturation in which translation plays such an important part. I shall be trying to analyse it for that reason, and I shall do so by using various translations of the *Kalevala*, a collection of Finnish oral poetry, which has been carefully constructed as the Finnish national epic on the analogy of the classical epic and, to some extent, also the Nordic sagas, as my example. The main thrust of the argument is that literatures written in languages that are less widely spoken, will only gain access to something that could be called 'world literature', if they submit to the textual system, the discursive formation, or whatever else one wants to call it, underlying the current concept of 'world literature'. They have, in other words, to create something that is analogous to some element of 'world literature' as it already exists, whether that element is actually part of their own literature in that form or not. In the nineteenth century, which is the time frame that concerns us here, that textual system was still markedly generic in nature. Modernism with its various concepts of collage and bricolage had not yet made its appearance on the scene, and Romanticism, which prided itself on having broken the yoke of neo-classical handbooks of poetics, still observed the difference between the epic, say, and the ode, or other genres. The *Kalevala* and its translations into English provide us with a very interesting case study of both conscious and subconscious submission to 'world literature'. By means of this case study I want to valorise the existence of both a textual system, some kind of 'grid' of accepted and acceptable text types that pre-exist language, and that decide whether a certain text is accepted or rejected by a certain culture, and a similar conceptual system for translation studies. Both textual system and conceptual grids may coincide with a language, or a nation, as is the case with Chinese and Japanese literature. More often than not, though, they pre-date more than one language, more than one nation. One could, in this context, speak of something like a 'Western' grid, whose existence is attested by the existence of the epic, for instance, in Greek, Latin, and a number of other languages, and by the existence of Romanticism, for instance, as a set of conceptual categories transcending various nations. One could also speak of Near Eastern grids, that would encompass the classical Arabic, Farsi, Ottoman, and even Urdu literatures and societies. In fact, the case of grids pre-dating different, sometimes radically different languages and societies is the prevalent one, since such grids can also be said to pre-date the various Indian and African languages, literatures, and societies. When the grids pre-date different languages, cultures, and societies, a type of genre developed in one literature, say the classical epic, can, and does, therefore, prescribe how works of literature written in another language have to be written, with respect to structure, diction, and other elements, whereas the dominant conceptual grid may well prescribe how something like the 'heroic age', in which epics were written, ought to be imagined. In choosing the *Kalevala* as my example, I am indeed banking heavily on the cross-cultural importance of these grids, not least because I am utterly ignorant of the language in which the *Kalevala* was written. Yet I maintain that the twin concepts of analogy and the grids are of such fundamental importance that they underwrite the validity and importance of the points I shall be making in what follows.

Before proceeding further, though, I want to make it very clear that my use of the word 'pre-date' in connection with the grids mentioned above, is not intended to have any overtones of the deconstructionist 'always already there'. The grids are not inevitable, and inevitably baked into whatever trace is left of whatever it was that may, presumably, almost have existed before human beings began to write. Rather, they are historical constructs, brought into being by certain relatively unmysterious and eminently 'traceable' forces, maintained for a certain span of time, and then changed, or abandoned.

The 'primal analogy' that started the whole process leading to the construction of the *Kalevala*, is described as follows by Keith Bosley (1989) in the introduction to his translation of that work:

> Scotland, still smarting after Culloden, had welcomed Ossian, while the response on the continent had amounted to a craze. Modern research has shown that the texts were based on genuine material, but that Mcpherson [*sic*] lacked the scholarship to do it justice. Such scholarship was, meanwhile, evolving on the other side of Europe, where the Finnish historian Henrik Gabriel Porthan and his students saw in Macpherson at least a kindred spirit. (xvi)

The point is that Scotland, which had seen its existence as an independent nation come to an end with the defeat at Culloden, tried to compensate by 'discovering' a national literature. This is not the place to go into the details of James Macpherson's manufacturing of Ossian, nor of any of the other texts he purportedly 'translated from the Gaelic or Erse language', as it says in the full title of his *Fragments of Ancient Poetry*, published in 1760. The salient fact for our argument is that if a nation wanted to be a nation in late eighteenth and, especially, in nineteenth-century Europe, it needed a national literature whose roots had to stretch back into 'the mists of time', or some such metaphor, particularly if that nation could not be a nation in the political sense, at least not entirely in the form in which it wanted to be.

Since a national literature had to stretch back into the mists of time, and since those mists had produced the genre of the epic in the oldest national literatures then known, both Greek and Sanskrit, new, hitherto unrecognised national literatures that wanted to be admitted to the fellowship of world literature, would considerably advance their case if they were able to produce an epic of their own. This is precisely what Macpherson set out to do for Scotland after the success of Ossian: he promised the Scottish Society an epic and delivered not one, but two epics in quick succession: *Finegal, an Ancient Epic Poem, in Six Books*, which appeared in 1762, and *Temora*, which was published a year later.

This was also what 'the Finnish historian Henrik Gabriel Porthan and his students' set out to do for Finnish. In the introduction to his translation of the *Kalevala*, Friberg (1988) overstates the case when he writes: 'the Finnish people through the Kalevala actually sang themselves into existence'. They did not sing themselves into existence, they were very consciously sung into existence as the result of a project envisaged by Porthan, fostered by Von Becker, and carried out by Lönnrot. Friberg's use of the word 'existence' above is symptomatic for the process I am trying to analyse here. By 'existence' he can only mean something like 'existence within the wider context of world literature', since the Finns themselves, presumably, were conscious of their own existence. The Porthan/Von Becker/Lönnrot project came into being because the Finns were no longer satisfied with existing 'for themselves;' rather, they wanted recognition by the outside world, the world of other nations and of 'world literature'.

Friberg correctly points out that the project to find or construct a Finnish national epic was symptomatic of 'the degree to which the nationalist movement had taken shape under the driving force of geopolitical changes, changes that then required a cultural response to fill the gap, rather than the other way around'. Though his statement is meant for Finland, it also applies to other nations. In fact, it is one of the key elements of the conceptual (as opposed to the textual) grid of Romanticism, which inspired nationalism all over Europe, and conjured up a vision of all nations, big or small, taking their place in the 'concert' of nations. The Scots had ceased to become an independent nation when Macpherson (who, it should also be remembered, published his own translation of the *Iliad* in 1773) constructed their epics for them, the Finns had not yet become one when Lönnrot did the same, in a climate in which 'the idea of a Finnish nation-state took root in Helsinki and St-Petersburg and its significance was grasped' (Branch, 1985: xxix). In both cases the people who constructed the epics were indeed 'concerned less with fidelity to sources than with the validation of a national culture' (Bosley, 1989: xvi), but that is where the similarity ends: far be it from me to suggest that Lönnrot would even have dreamed of treating the material he found in his travels all over Finland in the same way Macpherson treated the material he found, or pretended to find in the Highlands.

Two other points need to be made before we comment on Lönnrot's project in greater detail. One is that language played a much more ambiguous part in the construction and reconstruction of epics for use by nations whose languages are not widely spoken, than it did in the reconstruction of epics for nations whose languages were and are widely spoken. The first German philologists to edit the *Nibelungenlied*, for instance, were obviously able to do so in German. The Finnish scholars who wanted to (re)construct a Finnish national epic, on the other hand, were not able to discuss their project in the language whose long lost glory they set out to resurrect: 'with the exception of Von Becker, Lönnrot's teacher, the other early nationalists were forced of necessity to use Swedish — the only literary language known to them' (Friberg, 1988: 13). Similarly, the Finnish Literature Society, founded in 1831, 'had to write down its minutes in Swedish for decades, because none of its members knew enough Finnish' (Jänicke, 1991: 58). Language, in this case, as in that of many other smaller nations of Europe — the Czechs and the Flemings come to mind first — did not nearly play the role Romantic historiography — another discursive formation — has predisposed us to think it did. You could make plans for the revival of Finnish, Czech, and Flemish literature, but you made those plans in Swedish, German, and French. You could, in other words, try your best to conjure up the 'Geist' of the language to come; you were certainly not 'moved' by it as you went about the philological work necessary to provide that 'Geist' with a body.

The other point is that the actual readership of the national epic, within the nation, hardly matters. The insightful entry on the *Kalevala* by John H. Wuorinen in *Collier's Encyclopedia* sums up the situation as follows: 'While the intellectuals after 1835 hailed the Kalevala as a remarkable monument to the cultural heritage and achievement of the Finns in the distant past, it never became a people's book or treasure. (The first edition of five hundred copies sufficed for ten years)' (704a/b). But the *Kalevala* did not have to actually become a 'people's book'. It was enough that it was declared one. Since the requisite niche in the grid that regulated access to the 'concert' of nations had been filled, Finnish and the Finns could be admitted to its charmed circle while, for internal consumption, the *Kalevala*, once published, could be, and was 'cited in support of the cause of peace, the single tax, socialism, theosophy, and other isms' (Wuorinen 704b).

In his 1835 preface to the first version of his work, which has since become known as the *Old Kalevala*, Elias Lönnrot, who constructed the *Kalevala* on the basis of the oral poetry he collected all over Finland, but mainly in Karelia, wrote that he undertook the task of constructing the *Kalevala* because he wondered 'whether one might not possibly find songs about Väinämöinen, Ilmarinen, and Lemminkäinen, and other memorable forbears of ours until from these had been got longer accounts, too, just like the Greeks and the Icelanders and others got songs of their forebears' (translated in Magoun, 1963: 366). The model is clear, and it was definitely not Lönnrot's alone. In fact, Kaarle Akseli Gottlund had written in 1817: 'if one should desire to collect the old traditional songs and from these make a systematic whole, there might come from them an epic, a drama, or whatever, so that from this a new Homer, Ossian, or *Nibelungenlied* might come into being' (translated in Magoun, 1963: 350). Lönnrot set out to do precisely that: when he collected 'the old traditional songs' into a 'systematic whole', he did so with the analogue of the epic firmly in mind. 'In this', as Branch reminds us, 'he was also encouraged by contemporary theories about the compilation of the epics of classical Greek literature which suggested that "Homer" was the collector and arranger of local myths and tales rather than their creator' (xxx).

Although the analogue was clear, it was less clear whether the material could really be made to fit it. Lönnrot did his best, not least by eradicating from the folk poetry he collected all references to elements that would seem to contradict the claim that his epic under construction was firmly rooted in the mists of time: 'the frequent allusions in authentic materials to Christian features are notably absent from Lönnrot's epic; where they do occur, it is because Lönnrot did not perceive them as Christian in character' (Branch, 1985: xxxii). These allusions had been introduced into the authentic material Lönnrot collected by Christian missionaries and priests, who, from the twelfth century onward, 'did not hesitate to borrow the form and content of Kalevala poetry to communicate the new doctrine' (Branch, 1985:

xxv), using, in fact, that poetry as an analogue of their own, using the linguistic/literary grid to infiltrate new conceptual elements.

Lönnrot's most conscious and concentrated attempt to provide a classical/Nordic analogue occurs in the so-called 'Kullervo cycle', contained in runos 31–36 in the second, 1849 *Kalevala* edition. Kirby (1907) directs his readers' special attention to it in the preface to his translation, introducing it as 'a terrible tragedy, which has been compared to that of Oedipus' (xiii). To further reinforce the point, he makes use of the *Kalevala's* only English language analogue, stating that Kullervo 'is, in part, the prototype of Longfellow's "Kwasind"' (xiii). Not before 1985 does Branch abandon the analogy in his introduction to the latest re-edition of Kirby's highly successful translation, when he points out that 'the *Kullervo* cycle (Runos xxxi–xxxvi), which exerted an even greater influence on Finnish *fin de siècle* art and music, lacks a real counterpart in the authentic tradition' (xxxi). Rather, it is Lönnrot himself who has, in 1849, 'transformed Kullervo into a hero comparable to Oedipus and Hamlet' (xxxi), most likely because he thought such heroes would not be out of place in an epic worth its label. Again the power of analogy is illustrated by the fact that the influence of the Kullervo theme is authentic, and can be traced, has indeed become part of 'Finnish *fin de siècle* art and music', no matter whether that theme is actually there in the authentic material or not.

We have now come to the nodal point of the argument. Even though Lönnrot did all he could, the *Kalevala* is, in Magoun's words, 'really nothing like' (xiii) what has traditionally been associated with the classical epics, or even with the Nordic sagas, if one expects those works to exhibit something like 'a more or less unified and continuously moving plot with actors who are wealthy aristocratic warriors performing deeds of valour and displaying great personal resourcefulness and initiative, often, too, on a rather large scale' (xiii). Lönnrot, then, did not succeed in producing an epic on the classical/Nordic analogy, but that did, in the end, not matter to the outside world. Since Lönnrot had claimed the appellation 'epic' for his work, the outside world, to whose twin grids he had submitted, would oblige him, at least for about fifty years, what was left of the life span of the twin grids dominant when he began to work on the *Kalevala*, ignoring the fact that a description of the *Kalevala* as an epic 'has tended to do the work a certain disservice by raising expectations the reader is not likely to find fulfilled' (Magoun, 1963: xiii). With the exception of a few dissenting voices, what follows describes the process through which the *Kalevala*, in its first two English translations, and especially in the very first one, was turned into a much more obvious analogue of the classical/Nordic epic than Lönnrot's original ever succeeded in becoming. This successful 'analogisation', I claim, proves the overriding importance, not just of the generic system predominant in world literature from Lönnrot's times to the beginnings of modernism, but also the overriding importance of discursive formations, textual systems, grids, or whatnot, as such: the words used to designate the reality are not important; the reality itself is of the utmost importance since it displays, in the most obvious manner, the power of analogy, and in both directions. Since the dominant concept of 'world literature' of his time demanded that all national literatures should begin with epics, Lönnrot did what he could to oblige within the context of Finnish language and culture, by creating a passable analogue. Conversely, where that analogue was thought to be wanting, the dominant concept of 'world literature' would make it resemble even more what it wanted. Needless to say, the power of the textual system was aided and abetted in this by the fact that knowledge of Finnish was, and is, anything but widespread outside of Finland. For speakers of English who read the *Kalevala* in their language, the translation definitely functioned as an original. At no point, and by no stretch of the imagination, could Finnish be said to be a 'presence in the background' for readers of an English *Kalevala*, the way Latin and Greek were, at least until 1920, for readers of an English *Aeneid*, and English *Iliad*, or an English *Odyssey*.

Before I proceed to analyse this process of analogisation in more detail, fairness demands that I acknowledge at least two dissenting voices. Their very existence is also of the utmost importance: at no point do I want to give the impression that the influence exerted by the grids is all-pervasive and inescapable. It is great, but one can go against it. The fact that the grids do, eventually, change is the best proof of that. The whole process is by no means mechanistic, and should not be thought to be so. Let me give a trivial example from this very text. In this text I use the word 'analogue' throughout, even though the more Greek looking and sounding word 'analogon' also exists in English, and even though I might be thought to be more 'learned' if I used 'analogon' rather than 'analogue'. I use analogue precisely to indicate that I do not want to be categorised as belonging to a certain school for which I have very little sympathy.

The 1910 edition of the *Encyclopedia Britannica* did remark on the difference between the *Kalevala* and epics of the classical/Nordic type: 'while in the other antique epics of the world bloodshed takes a predominant place, the *Kalevala* is truly gentle, lyrical, and even domestic, dwelling at great length on situations of great beauty and romantic pathos' (Vol. 15, 640b). Similarly, Max Müller praised the *Kalevala* for 'equalling the *Iliad* in length and completeness', and then went on to say, another lone voice of dissent: 'nay, if we can forget for a moment all that we in our youth learned to call beautiful, no less beautiful. A Finn is not a Greek' (quoted in Crawford, 1888: xxxix).

The person who did most for the reception of the *Kalevala* by analogy, was its first translator into English, John Martin Crawford, who did not know Finnish, but based his translation on the translation into German published by Anton Schiefner in 1852, which is, to this day, one of two German translations that are actually based on the Finnish text, and which has been rewritten and adapted a fair number of times by others claiming to translate the *Kalevala* into German, not least among them Martin Buber. It is of the utmost importance to note here, unequivocally, that Crawford did not consciously set out to do so, at least not to the same extent Lönnrot consciously constructed his *Kalevala*. Rather, it is precisely because Craw- ford had internalised the twin grids dominating his age that he did what he did, that he thought it self-evident to do what he did, and that he thought what he did would greatly benefit the original he was translating.

Crawford prepares the reader in his long introduction. The *Kalevala*, he states unequivocally, is an epic, and as such it is 'true to the character of a national epic' in that it 'represents not only the poetry, but the entire wisdom and accumulated experience of a nation' (xliii). All the more reason, then, to acquaint the reader a little more with that nation. Not coincidentally, Crawford 's description of the Finns of his time seems designed to also evoke life in the simpler, 'heroic' times of their ancestors. 'Their temper is universally mild', (vi) the reader is told, they are 'happy-hearted' (vi), as well as being 'a cleanly people, much given to the use of vapor-baths' (vi). Finally, the (generic) Finn 'is not inhospitable, but not over-easy of access; nor is he a friend of new fashions' (vi). Not surprisingly for a fellow-believer in the strategy of analogy, Kirby also feels called upon to describe the Finns as 'a pious, industrious, and law-abiding people, the upper classes being highly educated' (vii).

The core of Crawford's strategy of analogy is to systematically equate what is in the *Kalevala* with its analogies in classical Greek mythology and literature. His most general statement, in this respect, is that 'the Finnish deities, like the ancient gods of Italy and Greece, are generally represented in pairs, and all gods are probably wedded' (xi). More specifically, the Finnish god Ukko is said to be 'like Atlas in the mythology of Greece', whereas 'we find the names Maa-emae (mother earth) and Maan-emo (mother of the earth) given to the Finnish Demeter' (Crawford, 1888: xx). The Finnish dead, not surprisingly, have to cross the 'Finnish Styx', (Crawford. 1888: xxvi) where the (unnamed) 'first daughter of Tuoni' ferries them across, 'like Charon, the son of Erebus and Nox, in the mythology of Greece' (Crawford, 1888: xxvii). Crawford's most specific, and easily most controversial equation is that of the mysterious 'sampo', which is never really described in detail or defined anywhere in the *Kalevala*, but is believed to be something like a pillar that holds up the very vault of the sky, with 'the Golden Fleece of the Argonautic expedition' (Crawford, 1888: xli). Significantly, in this context, the 1972 edition of the *Encyclopedia Britannica* no longer goes as far as Crawford, but still moves in the same direction, informing its readers that the 'sampo can be taken as the symbol of man's material and spiritual advancement' (Vol. 13, 191b). Crawford does not just equate characters and objects; he also goes into matters of structure: 'often too the unexpected is introduced after the manner of the Greek dramas, by a young child, or an old man' (xlii). The success of Crawford's strategy is attested to as late as 1953, when *Cassell's Encyclopedia of Literature* states that the *Kalevala* consists of 'the Odyssey-like quest of *sampo*, the magic mill, and the Iliad-like war between Kalevala (Finland) and Pohjola (Lapland, literally Northland)' (317a).

If the *Kalevala* is an epic, it must have a Homer-equivalent, and Kirby is happy to oblige with the following statement: 'it will be seen that Lönnrot edited the *Kalevala* from old ballads, much as the poems of Homer, or at least the *Iliad* and the *Odyssey*, are said to have been put together by order of Pisistratus' (viii). Crawford describes Lönnrot in some more detail, not surprisingly the kind of detail that fits the part. He describes him 'sitting by the fireside with the aged, rowing on the lakes with the fishermen, and following the flocks with the shepherds' (xxxvi), almost, but not quite, a father to his people, but definitely a scholar who 'so ingratiated himself into the hearts of the simple-minded people that they most willingly aided him in collecting these songs' (Crawford, 1888: xxxvi–xxxvii), even though we know from other sources that Lönnrot saw to it that the 'simple-minded people' always had enough alcohol to assist their memory. No wonder the national epic also makes its compiler into a national figure, certainly inside Finland. The Finnish literary encyclopedia *Iso Tietosanakirja* described Lönnrot as follows in its 1935 edition: 'as a human being Lönnrot is the epitome of a Finn, and, even if one tries, it is hard to find in him any objectionable traits; indefatigable assiduity and power of concentration, a quiet firmness and a kindly sense of humor under all circumstances, reasonableness and tolerance, extreme unpretentiousness, and truly Christian humility were characteristic of him' (translated in Magoun, 1963: 348).

On the level of the actual translation, the fact that the *Kalevala* is definitely an epic, and with a metre all its own, has its consequences. Crawford (1888) again projects the Finnish of his time (which he did not really know all that well) back into the epic mists of time, drawing an idealised picture: 'the natural speech of this people is poetry. The young men and maidens, the old men and matrons, in their interchange of ideas, unwittingly fall into verse. The genius of their language aids to this end, inasmuch as their words are strongly trochaic' (xlv). Needless to say, this metre has to be imitated in the translation, because it is part of the hallowed epic tradition as such, even though that imitation creates its own problems in practice, witness Kirby's somewhat more down to earth appraisal of the situation: 'the first syllable of every word is accented. This renders it difficult to accommodate such words as Kalevala to the metre. But I have tried to do my best' (viii), even though the problem is not limited to 'Kalevala' alone. Indeed, Kirby's (1907) 'chief difficulty has been to fit the Finnish names into even a simple English metre, so as to retain the correct pronunciation' (ix). Yet he insists he has succeeded better than 'Longfellow, whose "Song of Hiawatha" is only a rather poor imitation of the *Kalevala*' (Kirby, 1907: viii).

It is only after the textual system has been reshuffled, after World War I, that Magoun (1963) pleads for not imitating the metre of the original, arguing that 'more unfortunate than this rhythmical monotony is the highly restrictive nature of the measure, which allows a translator almost no latitude for rendering adequately or fully many verses in the original' (xvi). Bosley (1989) also abandons the metre of the original, appealing to history (which, in effect, amounts to invoking the authority of one textual system against another) as he does so: 'the present translation departs from the practice of many translators of the epic into many tongues by replacing the original metre with another... This, after all, has been the usual method in English since Gavin Douglas's *Aeneid*' (Bosley, 1989: xlvi). Accordingly, Bosley develops his own metre, 'like any metre evolved through the demands of translation — such as blank verse itself, invented by Surrey for translating Virgil' (Bosley, 1989: l). Friberg (1988) is somewhat less radical than Bosley, but he, too, 'has not hesitated ... to employ the occasional changes in the metrical pattern, avoiding the sometimes deadening monotony of Crawford's or Kirby's translations' (Schoolfield, 1988: 33).

It remains to finally turn to some instances taken from the translations themselves. I have limited these to a selection from Runo 13, which has widely divergent titles in the different translations. In Crawford it is called 'Lemminkäinen's Second Wooing', in keeping with the more elevated diction he uses throughout, to further strengthen the analogy with the epic, if not of Homer, then at least of Homer's Victorian translators. Kirby calls it 'Hiisi's Elk', betting on the exotic proper name for something like an epic effect. Magoun calls it 'Poem 13', in a somewhat pedestrian fashion, Bosley calls it 'The Demon's Elk', and Friberg calls it 'The Elk Chase' in keeping with his own strategy, which is defined by contrast with his older predecessors: 'the previous English translations have managed to disguise many of the poem's charms, including its homelier and funnier ones; the translators have not always felt at ease with the text, and have taken it, perhaps, almost too seriously' (Schoolfield, 1988: 38). It would, as I hope to have shown, be closer to the truth to say that translators like Crawford and, to a lesser extent, Kirby, had no choice but to take the poem very seriously as soon as they had passed through the grid of the textual system of their time. The epic is not supposed to be funny, and certainly not homely. If these characteristics unfortunately tend to surface in an original that is called 'epic' after all, they will certainly not penetrate into the translations. Once the textual system changes, though, Bosley can write in his preface '*Kalevala* has elements of subject and a general atmosphere that are not found in epic and romance as I know them in the European tradition from Homer through the eighteenth century' (vii).

A comparison of one of those elements, a few 'homely' lines in the different translations, will make different strategies behind those translations more obvious, and not just the strategies, but also the extent to which they have been dictated by textual systems. Throughout Runo 13, the protagonist, Lemminkäinen, who is called 'ancient' by Crawford (1888: 175), chases an elk to give it as a dowry to the woman Crawford calls 'the hostess of Pohjola' (175), in exchange for one of her 'winsome maiden[s]' (175) in Crawford's translation. In Kirby's translation they have become 'lovely daughter[s]' (130), 'maidens' (76) in Magoun's translation, 'wenches' (147) in Bosley's, and 'girls' (116) in Friberg's. Similarly, Lemminkäinen is 'lively' in Kirby, 'reckless' in Magoun, 'wanton' in Bosley, and 'wayward' in Friberg, no doubt because the meaning of the original word in Finnish is not entirely clear. In Kirby Crawford's 'hostess' has become 'Pohjola's old mistress;' in Magoun she is 'the Dame of North Farm', in Bosley 'the hag of Northland', and in Friberg 'the Dame of Pohjola'.

Since Lemminkäinen is going to chase an elk, it stands to reason that he will need snowshoes, not exactly the most heroic piece of equipment if one compares them to, for instance, the shield of Achilles in the *Iliad*. Yet, Crawford does his best when he is describing the way the snowshoes are made: 'Then he fastened well the shoe-straps,/Smooth as adder's skin the woodwork,/Soft as fox-fur were the stick rings' (179). Kirby changes the adder into an 'otter', and writes: 'Frames he lined with skins of otter/And the rings with ruddy foxskin' (131). Both emphasise the craftsmanship displayed by Lyylikki, the snow-shoe maker, who becomes a kind of Arctic Hephaistos, to take a leaf from Crawford's book, but the original does not care about the craftsmanship itself, but rather about what the craftsman will be paid, for his labour, again one of those mundane facts of life that are not easily integrated into an epic. Under the dispensation of a different textual system, though, Magoun translates 'the shaft of the pole cost an otter-skin/the disk a reddish foxskin' (77), Bosley writes 'the pole shaft cost an otter/and the snow-disc a brown fox' (149), and Friberg: 'for the pole an otterskin/for the disk a red fox [he] paid' (116).

Crawford's high diction also asserts itself in simple descriptions. Where he sees 'not a fleet deer of the forest' (178), both Kirby and Friberg see 'not a single four-foot runner'(132/117), Magoun sees 'anything running on four legs', (77) and Bosley sees '[something] running on four feet' (147).

Similarly, when Lyylikki warns Lemminkäinen that his chances of success are rather slim, Crawford produces something full of epic doom with a hint of the exotic: 'Thou wilt catch but pain and torture/In the Hisi fens and forests' (177). Kirby writes 'For a piece of rotten timber/Only will reward your labour' (131), which is considerably simpler, but by no means as ominous, as Crawford's translation. Magoun stays close to Kirby: 'You will get a piece of rotten wood/and that with a lot of misery' (76). Bosley stays close to both: ''tis a scrap of rotten wood/you'll get, and that with great grief' (148). Friberg strikes out on his own, writing: 'You'll get nothing for your pains/but a hollow hunk of punkwood' (116), and adding in a footnote: 'The ski-maker gives fair warning: he knows the tricks of which the demons are capable. They can create the illusion in a hunter's mind that he sees an elk, hunts it down and kills it, only to find an old decayed tree stump in place of the carcass' (116). The footnote makes the plot of the story much clearer to a reader unfamiliar with Finnish demons of the heroic age and the tricks they were up to.

Toward the end of Runo 13 Lemminkäinen captures what Crawford calls a 'wild-moose' (182). Kirby and Magoun a 'reindeer' (135/79) and Bosley and Friberg an 'elk' (153/119). Only in Crawford's translation is it actually stated that he 'spake again [to the wild-moose] in measured accents' (182). In the other translations he just speaks to the animal without further authorial intervention. Now that he has captured the animal, and therefore the dowry, Lemminkäinen thinks of what will happen when he gives the dowry to the old woman. Crawford has him say: 'I would like a while to linger,/I would like to rest a moment/In the cottage of my maiden,/With my virgin, young and lovely' (182). Kirby even heightens the epic diction, or rather, makes it sound more like Victorian *Iliads*, *Odysseys*, and *Aeneids*. His first two lines read: 'Would that I awhile might tarry,/And might sleep awhile and rest me', (135). In his last line he introduces an element that is not there in Crawford's translation: 'Here beside a youthful maiden,/With a dove of blooming beauty' (135). The dove, obviously Kirby's epic transfiguration of a lowlier bird, becomes 'a chick who was growing up'

(79) in Magoun's translation, in keeping with his stated strategy, which holds that 'a simple, straightforward, and dignified language seems to be in order, with minimal use of bookish words or exalted language and without slang, though in many dialogues a thoroughly colloquial idiom seems appropriate' (xvi). If the 'bookish words' and 'exalted language' are directed against Magoun's two predecessors, the 'slang' may well be directed against his two successors, even though he should approve of Bosley's first two lines: 'this is just the place for me/just the right place to lie down' (153). Friberg tries to keep to the use of straightforward language, but with a phonetic layer over it designed to reproduce if not the sounds of the original, at least their effects: 'There's a soft bed for me here;/What a smooth pad that, to lie on' (119). Friberg's chick is 'just budding out', 119, whereas Bosley has, perhaps somewhat unfortunately: 'beside a young maid/with a growing hen' (153).

It is rather obvious that Crawford consistently walks the high road throughout, both in his introduction and in his translation. Kirby follows him relatively closely in doing so, although he also states that '*Kalevala* contains many beautiful passages and episodes which are by no means inferior to those we find in the ballad-literature of better-known countries than Finland' (xiv), suggesting that the *Kalevala*, while obviously an epic, is also, at least to some extent, an epic not exactly on the classical/Nordic model. He will therefore not always use the 'exalted language' that is Crawford's trademark, but he will do so more often than not. Obviously, both that 'exalted language' and words more readily identified as 'bookish' are hard to find in the translations made by Magoun, Bosley, and Friberg.

I have already made the point that the translators had little choice in the matter, that they had (and have) to conform to the textual system of their time if they want to be read or heard. It is not hard to imagine, for instance, that no publisher would have published Bosley's translation, or even Magoun's in 1888. What they, and Friberg wrote would, in our imaginary publisher's frame of reference, quite simply not qualify as an 'epic'. What matters, then, in these translations as in many others, is not primarily knowledge, or even mastery of languages, but rather submission to textual and conceptual grids.

References

Bosley, Keith (1989) *The Kalevala*. Oxford: Oxford University Press.
Branch, M.A. (1985) Introduction. In W.F. Kirby *Kalevala. The Land of Heroes* (pp. i–xxxv). London and Dover, NH: The Athlone Press.
Cassell's Encyclopedia of Literature (1953) London: Cassell.
Crawford, John Martin (1888) *The Kalevala*. New York: John B. Alden.

Encyclopedia Britannica, Eleventh edition (1910). Cambridge: Cambridge University Press.

Encyclopedia Brittanica, Fourteenth edition (1972). Chicago and London: William Benton.

Friberg, B. (1988) *The Kalevala.* Helsinki: Otava Publishing Company Ltd.

Jänicke, Gisbert (1991) *Kalevaland.* Hamburg: Helmut Buske.

Kirby, W.F. (1907) *Kalevala. The Land of Heroes.* London and New York: Dent and Dutton.

Magoun, Francis Peabody, Jr (1963) *The Kalevala.* Cambridge, MA: Harvard University Press.

Schoolfield, George (1988) Introduction. In Eino Friberg *The Kalevala* (pp. 26–38). Helsinki: Otava Publishing Company Ltd.

Wuorinen, John H. Kalevala. In *Colliers Encyclopedia* (Vol. 13, 704). New York and Toronto: Macmillan.

Chapter 6

Still Trapped in the Labyrinth: Further Reflections on Translation and Theatre

SUSAN BASSNETT

In 1985 I published an essay entitled 'Ways through the Labyrinth', subtitled 'Strategies and Methods of Translating Theatre Texts'. That essay represented a way-station on what has been a long, tortuous journey that started in the mid-1970s and is still going on even as we come to the end of the century. Over the years I have revised my views several times, though I still find that the image of the labyrinth is an apt one for this most problematic and neglected area of translation studies research. Less has been written on the problems of translating theatre texts than on translating any other text type.

It is generally accepted that the absence of theory in this area is connected to the nature of the playtext itself, which exists in a dialectical relationship with the performance of that same text. There is a large body of work that seeks to investigate the relationship between the written play and its performance, though much of this is either descriptive or speculative. The labyrinthine difficulties of describing and analysing what takes place when a playtext is transposed from one language into another and performed in that second language extend the problematics of the relationship between play and performance much further and compound the problems. This essay will explore some of those complexities.

Subtext/Gestic Text/Inner Text

In his book *Transposing Drama*, Egil Tornqvist (1991) declares that translation theorists have almost completely disregarded the problem of whether the acting subtext that can be deduced from the source text can also be deduced from the target texts. Ironically, this is precisely where I started too, in an early essay that struggled to discuss the Stanislawskian subtext in terms of translation (Bassnett, 1978). The answer, of course, is that this is an impossibility: if such a thing as a subtext exists at all, it will inevitably be decoded in different ways by different performers, for there can be no such thing as a single, definitive authoritative reading, despite the fact that some authors think there should be. Chekhov, for example, wished he could have prevented his plays from being translated and performed outside Russia, because audiences would not have access to the specifically Russian codes embedded in his writing. Had his wish come true, we should have been deprived of the very English Chekhovian tradition that sees his work through the filter of the English class system. Equally, Pirandello raged against what he saw as the betrayal of his plays, not only by translators but in the first instance by actors:

> How many times does some poor dramatic writer not shout 'No, not like that!' when he is attending rehearsals and writhing in agony, contempt, rage and pain because the translation into material reality (which, perforce, is someone else's) does not correspond to the ideal conception and execution that had begun with him and belonged to him alone. (Pirandello, 1908)

Pirandello saw the playtext as belonging principally to the author, so that the performance was seen as an attack upon that author's intentions because it was no more than a copy. This is obviously an extreme position, but it raises the fundamental question of the relationship between the written playtext and any eventual translation of it, be that translation interlingual or intersemiotic, i.e. into performance. This question dogs theatre analysts and semioticians, just as much as it dogs translation scholars and translators. We may not share Pirandello's archaic view of the writer as owner of a text, but we do not have an adequate theory of the playtext which would enable us to view the relationship between play and performance in new terms and offer a counter-position to his notion of betrayal.

A great deal of the language about translation concerns loss. We are told that things get lost in translation, that a translation is second-best, a pale copy of the original. This discourse of loss dominates much discussion of the translation of poetry and prose, but curiously in theatre the idea of loss is usually reversed. What we have instead is the notion of the playtext that is somehow incomplete in itself until realised in performance. The play is therefore something that fails to achieve wholeness until it is made physical.

Anne Ubersfeld has argued that the playtext is *troué*, it is full of gaps that can only be realised physically (Ubersfeld, 1978). Others have seen the playtext as a network of latent signs, waiting to be brought out in performance, as the deep structure of a performance, or even as a blueprint for an eventual performance. What all these theories have in common is the idea that the play is not complete in itself and requires a physical dimension for its full potential to be realised. One line of enquiry in theatre semiotics has concerned itself with that relationship between the written and the eventual physicalising of the written. Theories of acting, from Stanislawski through Brecht, have evolved the notion of the gestic text that is somehow encoded in the written and can then be deciphered by an actor.

If there is gestic text, or inner text that is read intuitively by actors and directors as they begin to build a performance, we need to ask whether that text will be a constant or will it vary? Translation suggests that it would have to be infinitely variable. For if we have five different versions of the same playtext, we presumably have five different gestic texts. How can there ever be any certainty about whether the inner text decoded by actors in the source culture will be the same as that decoded in the target culture? Theatres are not consistent, conventions vary radically from culture to culture. Stanislawski's reading of *Othello*, for example, where he suggests that Desdemona deserved a slap from her husband for interfering, would be deemed unacceptably sexist today.

On my journey through the labyrinth, I have argued that if we accept the idea of a gestic text that exists within a written text and needs excavating by actors, then we are faced with an absurd problem for translators (Bassnett, 1991). For the translator is effectively being asked to do the impossible. If the written text is merely a blueprint, a unit in a complex of sign systems including paralinguistic and kinesic signs, and if it contains some secret gestic code that needs to be realised in performance, then how can the translator be expected not only to decode those secret signs in the source language, but also to re-encode them in the target language ? Such an expectation does not make sense. To do such a thing a translator would not only have to know both languages and theatrical systems intimately, but would also have to have experience of gestic readings and training as a performer or director in those two systems.

Acculturating the Playtext

Marvin Carlson suggests that this problem has a long history, and traces it back to the late eighteenth century when performance was effectively seen as *illustration*. He cites Charles Lamb's famous remark on 'how much *Hamlet* is changed into another thing by being acted' (Carlson, 1985). It is precisely this changing into another thing to which Pirandello objects, even while recognising the impossibility of tying any text to any single reading. How much more of another thing was Ducis' French version of *Hamlet*, produced in 1770! In a letter to Garrick of the same year, Ducis explained that he had been unable to include the character of the ghost, which would have offended good taste (he also removed the players, the combat scene between Hamlet and Laertes and some fifteen characters):

> So I was forced, in a way, to create a new play. I just tried to make an interesting character of the parricidal queen and above all to depict the pure and melancholic Hamlet as a model of filial tenderness. (Heylen, 1993)

Ducis' letter raises another major issue that affects the translation of theatre texts: the expectations of the target audience and the constraints imposed by the target theatrical system. Romy Heylen has suggested that in translation there is a sliding scale of acculturation that runs from one extreme, where no attempt is made to acculturate the source text that may result in the text being perceived as 'exotic' or 'bizarre', through a middle stage of negotiation and compromise, and finally to the opposite pole of complete acculturation. But Sirkuu Aaltonen argues that acculturation is inevitable in the translation of a playtext and certainly if that written text is seen as one element in the total process that makes up theatre, then it would follow that some degree of acculturation cannot be avoided and is perhaps more visible than with other types of text (Aaltonen, 1996). Ducis' rewriting of *Hamlet* in accordance with French taste is a classic case of acculturation, for norms of taste prohibited a complete rendering of Shakespeare's play. Nevertheless, norms of taste in eighteenth-century England did not judge Shakespeare as acceptable either, so in both native performances of some of his plays at that time and in translations we find radical cuts, additions and revisions in order better to accommodate the demands of the target audience.

Translation never takes place in a vacuum; it always happens in a continuum, and the context in which the translation takes place necessarily affects how the translation is made. Just as the norms and constraints of the source culture play their part in the creation of the source text, so the norms and conventions of the target culture play their inevitable role in the creation of the translation. The anglicisation of Chekhov, referred to above, is a case in point, though some translators go so far as to deny Chekhov's cultural origins and claim him as an honorary Englishman.

Michael Frayn, for example, in a debate on theatre translation at the Lyttleton Theatre in October 1989, declared that Chekhov is universal:

> The good thing about Chekhov is that you don't need to know a word of Russian to be able to translate his plays because everyone knows what Chekhov is about, everyone knows by some sort of inner certainty what Chekhov intended and what he was saying, and the idea of referring it to some original text is absolutely odious.

Frayn has, with astonishing arrogance, assumed that the English language world can access the Russian regardless of linguistic or cultural difference. 'Everyone', he claims, understands Chekhov, and understands not only the plays as written, but also the author's intentions.

Others have questioned quite who is meant by 'everyone'. In his preface to his translation of *The Cherry Orchard* in 1978, Trevor Griffiths discusses how Chekhov's texts have been transformed into lyrical, nostalgic evocations of an idealised time past:

> Chekhov's tough, bright-eyed complexity was dulced into swallowable sacs of sentimental morality ... Translation followed translation, *that* idiom became 'our' idiom, that class 'our' class, until the play's specific historicity and precise sociological imagination had been bleached of all meanings beyond those required to convey the necessary 'natural' sense that the fine will always be undermined by the crude and that the 'human condition' can for all essential purposes be equated with 'the plight of the middle classes'.

Griffiths' point is that English translations of Chekhov have established a conventional way of reading his works that has resulted in a major shift of meaning and an alteration of the ideological basis of Chekhov's thinking. The acculturation process has domesticised the Russian writer and shifted the focus away from the Russian-bound aspects of his work. What we have, therefore, is not a Russian but an English Chekhov, or rather, an English middle-class Chekhov, and it is this playwright, invented through the translation process, whose work has entered the English literary system. It is difficult to imagine how any gestic subtext encoded in a Russian or English version of Chekhov could ever be remotely comparable, given the vastness of cultural difference.

'Performability'

The process of transposing a written text into performance is often referred to in English as a 'translation'. The use of this term can cause a certain confusion, for this would imply that a performance of a translated text in the target culture is then a translation of a translation. We can perhaps explain this usage by the absence in English of terms in common currency in other languages such as *mise en scène*, that refers to the process of putting on a performance, *spectacle* which can also be crudely translated as 'performance' or *scenario*, that refers to the text used by commedia dell'arte performers (and others) as the basis for their improvisations. These terms are left untranslated in English, which testifies to the differences in theatre tradition and practice between the English theatre and the French or Italian. In the absence of a coherent terminology of its own, English has tended to confound the act of translating a playtext across languages with the act of transposing a written text onto the stage. Discussion of the problems of translating theatre texts has tended to confuse these two quite separate processes.

One aspect of that confusion has been the continued emphasis on the notion of 'performability' or 'speakability' which is often perceived as a prerequisite for a theatre translation. I have great problems with 'performability'. It seems to me a term that has no credibility, because it is resistant to any form of definition. It is often used by reviewers to evaluate translations, when it is claimed that a translation by x is somehow more 'performable' than the translation produced by y. It may, of course, be true that one translation works better than another, but there will always be many factors involved which can range from simple incompetence on the part of a translator to changes in the expectations of the target readership and divergence in theatre or social systems. 'Performability' is a term that has found its way into many translators' prefaces, where it is often suggested that the translated text may be more congenial to an eventual performance because it is somehow more readily performable. We are always expected to take such statements at face value, since there is never any indication of what 'performable' means and why one text should be more performable than another.

On another stage of my journey through the labyrinth, I explored the history of the notion of performability as a criterion for evaluating a translation. The explanation I proposed for its emergence and continued use is due in part to the paucity of theoretical work on the relationship between the written text and performance, which means that we have no clear definition of what a performable text is (Bassnett, 1991). Then there is the relative absence of theoretical writing on theatre and translation. It is also significant that the term 'performability' appears to emerge at the same time as the naturalist drama, and is consequently linked to ideas of consistency in characterisation and to the notion of the gestural subtext. That consistency in characterisation is a recent convention does not seem to have been taken much into account, and we shall return to this point later when looking at Shakespeare's *Richard II*.

André Lefevere has pointed out that there is an almost complete lack of work on the staging of translations:

> Although many monographs of X as translator of Y exist in the field of drama translation, none to my knowledge go beyond treating drama as simply the text on the page. There is therefore practically no theoretical literature on the translation of drama as acted and produced. (Lefevere, 1992)

In this void, 'performability' as a criterion for translators who express concern about the problem of remaining faithful to an original has crept into use. The translator of dramatic texts is expected to grapple not only with the eternal problem of 'faithfulness', however that may be interpreted, but also with the problem of what the relationship between the written and the performed may be. 'Performability' offers a way out of the dilemma, since it allows the translator to take greater liberties with the text than many might deem acceptable, in the interests of the end product of 'performability'. The term thus justifies translation strategies, in much the same way as terms such as 'adaptation' or 'version' which have never been clearly defined either, are also used to justify or explain certain strategies that may involve degrees of divergence from the source text.

A few years ago David Hirst and I translated Pirandello's *Trovarsi* for BBC Radio (Bassnett & Hirst, 1987). The play presented a lot of problems, many of which were concerned with register. Set in the 1920s, it is the story of an actress, Donata Genzi, who is hugely successful but who has no clear sense of her self. On a visit to a friend's house, she falls in love with a young man, Elj Nielsen, after a night out at sea in a storm during which both of them have nearly drowned. Donata realises she is genuinely in love with Elj, but he hates the theatre, and when he sees her perform, repeating in front of the public the same loving gestures he thought were for him alone, he demands that she chose between life with him and her life as an actress. In a powerful monologue in the final act, Donata relives a scene from the play that has been her great triumph, recognising the bitter irony of being able to appear more real when performing than in her own life. As she speaks, the stage dissolves from an hotel bedroom into an auditorium, in a coup de théâtre that demonstrates the influence of expressionist staging techniques upon Pirandello's later plays.

The principal problem for the translators was the register: all the characters belong to the lesser nobility, and the play is set in the 1920s. It was difficult to avoid parodic language of the P. G. Wodehouse variety, (i.e. a fake 1920s English) while ensuring that some sense of period was retained. Such difficulties are part and parcel of any translation process, and we both sought to resolve them as best we could. But in addition to the questions of style and register were the constraints of radio. Pirandello had written his play for performance in a theatre. Its English premiere, however, was to be on the radio. We coped with this in several ways: names were added to the dialogue, so that it would be clear to listeners who was speaking to whom, and occasionally lines were inserted into the text to clarify a visual signal. When Donata first meets Elj, for example, she is symbolically dressed in green, so we added a line in which Elj compliments her on her choice of colour. But the biggest obstacle remained the final scene, when the hotel room is transformed into an auditorium and the impact for the spectator is heightened by this impressive visual alteration.

The solution we found was to reshape the final scene, transposing visual effects into verbal. So, for example, we intercut a dialogue between Donata, her friend Elisa, Elj's uncle, Count Mola and Giviero with parts of the final monologue in which Donata relives her role. The Italian has Donata alone in front of a mirror, going over the lines as she takes off her makeup :

> Coi deboli non si può essere pietosi. E allora, cacciala, cacciala via.
> (One cannot show any mercy to people who are weak. So throw her out! Throw her out of here!)
> *Tra se, come non contenta del tono con cui ha detto la stessa frase*
> *(To herself, as though she is not happy with the way she delivered that line)*
> Cacciala via! Cacciala via! E lei stessa, lo vedi? a volermi crudele!- Ma vi pare che lui possa esitare, tra me e voi?
> So, signora, so la vostra grande nobiltà, la levigatura che ne ...'
> (Throw her out! Don't you realize that she is the one who has made me so cruel? - How could you think he would have any hesitation in choosing between us? I am well, aware, signora, of your social status and the way you
> *arresto di memoria*
> *(her memory falters)*
> No, com'è?
> (No, how did it go?)
> Come ripassandosi ora la parte, senz'alcun tono
> *(Running through the part now, without any expression)*
> 'che ne vieni', sì ...
> (the way you smoothe over, yes that's it)

The English version moved this part of the speech earlier in the scene, and intercut it with dialogue with the other characters. So the scene went as follows:

Donata: One cannot show any mercy to people who are weak. So throw her out! Throw her out of here!

Elisa: Donata dear, what are you talking about? Who do you want thrown out?

Donata: *(continues in the same vein)* Throw her out! Don't you realize that she is the one who has made me so cruel? How could you think he would have any hesitation in choosing between us?

Elisa: Donata, Donata what is it? Are you alright?

Donata: Oh yes, Elisa, I've never been more 'alright' in my life.

Elisa: Who do you want thrown out then?

Donata: That other woman. My rival of course. You've already forgotten
          the play, haven't you? What I say in the third act: 'Throw her
          out, one cannot show any mercy to people who are weak', that
          was the turning point for me, the beginning of my own sense of
          freedom.

By this process of cutting and pasting lines from different parts of the
final scene, the denouement, in which the actress discovers her own
freedom (and simultaneously her own eternal imprisonment) by recognising that she is doomed forever to live as an actress and not as a real woman
was made accessible for the radio audience. Elisa served as Donata's mirror,
reflecting for listeners what was going on in Donata's mind and which a
stage audience would have seen rendered in physical action. But my point
in citing this strategy here is that I would strenuously resist the application
of any term such as 'adaptation' or 'version' to our translation, with their
concomitant implications that an adaptation or version depart more
radically from the source text than does a translation. What we did was to
take into account the constraints not only of source and target languages
and contexts, but also of the medium. Radio performance and theatre
performance are not the same, for the pattern of sign systems is fundamentally different. Ours was therefore a translation that took on board a number
of textual and extratextual factors and sought solutions through language.

Drama as Literature

It is significant that the criterion of 'performability' has not been
universally applied, so that some translations are deemed more performable than others. Distinctions have sometimes been drawn between
translations produced for a reading public and translations produced with
some ultimate idea of performance. This creates a curious distinction, for,
as Jiři Veltrusky points out, not all plays are written exclusively for
performance, and often other types of text can be performed:

> Sometimes, though less frequently, works of lyric, and narrative
> literature too, fulfill that function. Therefore, those who declare that the
> specific characteristic of drama consists in its link with acting are
> mistaken. Such a criterion is not only far from being pertinent, it is not
> even useful as a practical tool for a first approach ... Theatre is not
> another literary genre but another art. It uses language as one of its
> materials while for all the other literary genres, including drama,
> language is the only material — though each organizes it in a different
> fashion. (Veltrusky, 1977)

Veltrusky is here distinguishing between drama and theatre. He perceives drama as a genre and a dramatic text as one that is written to be read within the conventions of the genre. But the eventual relationship with performance remains outside its generic boundaries. Veltrusky makes a strong case for drama as literature in the first instance. He argues that drama can emerge from and dissolve into lyric or narrative, as is the case of much medieval writing. He points out that many plays have been written not for theatrical performance but only to be read, and we may include texts like Hardy's *The Dynasts* or Byron's *Manfred* here. Furthermore, he argues, dramatic texts are frequently read:

> all plays, not only closet plays, are read by the public in the same way as poems and novels. The reader has neither the actors nor the stage but only language in front of him. Quite often he does not imagine the characters as stage figures or the place of action as a scenic set. Even if he does, the difference between drama and theatre remains intact, because the stage figures and scenic sets are then immaterial meanings whereas in theatre they are material bearers of meaning.

Sign Systems and Performance

Tadeusz Kowzan famously defines five categories of expression in the making of a performance, which correspond to five semiotic systems (Kowzan, 1975). The first of these is the spoken text, for which there may or may not be a written script, the second is bodily expression, the third the actor's external appearances, gestures etc. , the fourth is the playing space with props, lighting etc. and the fifth is non-spoken sound. From these five categories, he determines 13 distinct subsections, and this basic structuralist map of performance, though modified from time to time, by others, remains a useful tool for understanding the complex interrelationship between sign systems in theatre. The spoken text is only one component, and the written text, if there is one at all, exists within the system of the verbal only.

Once we accept that the written text is not fundamental to performance but is merely one element in an eventual performance, then this means that the translator, like the writer, need not be concerned with how that written text is going to integrate into the other sign systems. That is a task for the director and the actors and serves again to underline the fact that theatre is a collaborative process in which not only are different sign systems involved, but a host of different people with different skills.

Veltrusky argues that we need to look at the dramatic text as literature, and this seems a helpful starting point for the translator. In the case of *Trovarsi*, described above, the translators had the specific brief of making the play suitable for radio, which also involved bearing in mind the time scheduled for the broadcast and amending the text accordingly. But the translator's task involves the interlingual transfer of a piece of writing, and speculation about the possible existence of coded gestic texts or a feature termed 'performability' or 'speakability' will not take us very far.

Reading a Playtext

For a start, the term 'play' refers to a text that may have been created in very different ways. We can say that a play consists basically of dialogue and stage directions, but beyond that consensus is difficult. In some cases, the text we end up with has been devised during rehearsals and changed frequently in performance. This type of dramatic text, published after a performance, has generally been edited, stage directions may have been added, decisions have been taken as to which parts shall remain in the printed version. This is the case of a great many published versions of successful alternative theatre performances, and it is also what happened to Shakespeare's texts, which were originally devised for and during performance and written down and edited later.

Alternatively, we may have a dramatic text written in the form of a play but not intended for performance at all. Or we may have a dramatic text that contains such detailed stage directions and portraits of characters that it serves a double function: on the one hand it may well be intended for performance, but on the other hand it is also aimed at readers. From Bernard Shaw to Arnold Wesker, naturalist dramas contain extended narrative sequences that help readers to locate themselves vis a vis the plot and characters. We may well ask for whom is the following detailed description from Act I of *Trovarsi* intended:

Marchesa Boveno and her granddaughter Nina come in. The Marchesa is a massive, heavy woman but a real lady. Her grandaughter is a lively, sharp-featured tomboy, with inquisitive eyes and a small straight nose that sniffs and ferrets into everything. Nina is distressed and irritated by her doll-like shortness, which is inclined to spread into the curvaceousness of a woman rather than the sinuous lines of a girl. They treat her like a child, as someone rather silly, and this constantly annoys her. Nina would like to be a trendy young woman. Her grandmother who is also rather comical with her antiquated pronouncements of wisdom is open-minded but keeps her on a tight rein. Both women enter wrapped in shawls. The Marchesa wears a hat, Nina is bareheaded. The older woman is out of breath.

Veltrusky suggests that such stage directions, which are effectively the author's notes and comments, are designed primarily for readers and disappear in performance, when they are replaced by other signs. A text such as the above is essentially literary and signals the presence of the playwright within the play, making him or her visible to a reader.

There are, moreover, a whole range of different ways of reading of a playtext. We might consider the following broad categories:

(1) The play read solely as literature, unrelated to any possible or remembered performance. This is frequently the way plays are taught in schools or universities.

(2) The post-performance reading, when the recollection of a performance seen is encoded into the private reading.

(3) The director's reading, which may involve a process of decision making as to whether the play will be performed or not. In such a reading, the constraints and possibilities offered by the text would be foregrounded in the director's interpretation of it.

(4) The actor's reading, which would focus on a specific role, perhaps to the degree of erasing other roles. If we look at performance scripts marked by actors, then an individual's role is highlighted and other roles perceived as secondary or instrumental.

(5) The designer's reading, which would involve a visualisation of spatial and physical dimensions that the text may open up.

(6) To these we might add the dramaturgical reading, and readings by any other individual or group involved in the production process.

(7) The rehearsal reading, which is subsequent to initial readings and will involve an aural, performance element through the use of paralinguistic signs such as tone, inflexion, pitch, register etc.

There is therefore a notion of multiplicity in the act of reading a playtext with an eventual performance in mind that corresponds to the notion of multiplicity in performances of that text. There is also a distinction to be made between these readings and the private, non-performance-oriented readings.

The translator's reading may interconnect to any of the above, but will inevitably differ because the translator's primary task is the ultimate rendering of the text into another linguistic system. But the translator needs to bear in mind the circumstances surrounding the production of the text in the first place. So, for example, in the case of Pirandello, we have a writer who deliberately structured his plays for private reading as well as for performance, and who demanded that his instructions be followed scrupulously, whilst in the case of Shakespeare, we have the phenomenon of a collection of texts that have become canonical only through the work of editors and critics, since their original devising was a collaborative, improvisational project. The way in which the parts are distributed to the Mechanicals in *A Midsummer Night's Dream*, or to the Players in *Hamlet* offers a graphic illustration of how English Renaissance actors treated the printed word. The similarities between this method of devising a play and the commedia dell'arte *scenario* is immediately apparent. In neither case was the text written to be read.

The collaborative nature of early dramas can be seen in their lack of consistency. The naturalist drama saw consistency of plot and characterisation as important, and the received idea of a play that prevails today still tends towards this assumption. Yet if we consider Shakespeare as an example, seen by many as a supreme depicter of character, consistency is not important, and it is the translation reading that brings this out most clearly. Let us take as an example *Richard II*. This play, one of Shakespeare's histories, traces the fall of Richard and the rise of Bolingbroke, as issues of good and bad government are explored and the relationship between individual morality and the good of the state is called into question from different perspectives. The imagery of the play is heavily symbolic: images of rising and falling, the turning of Fortune's wheel, combine with images that contrast a well-kept and an unkempt garden, nature wild and nature carefully nurtured. The play is constructed around a series of pageant-like scenes, and contains a great deal of reported speech, since Richard is constantly presented to the audience through the opinions of different characters, some for him some violently against him.

The character of Richard has been much debated by critics and actors. In the first part of the play he wavers, unable to take sensible decisions and prove his worth as a king. But as the action progresses and the forces of change begin to move him away from the seat of power he becomes increasingly articulate about his plight, and has at times been seen as a Christ-like figure in his final agony. However actors chose to portray Richard, the fact is that like most Shakespearean drama, characterisation takes place on the level not of action but of language. Hence if we apply naturalist criteria, Richard's character is inconsistent in this play — he starts out feebly and metamorphoses into a tragic hero. But if we apply Renaissance criteria, and conceive of character as evolving through language, then such inconsistencies in the text are entirely explicable. Here is Richard in Act I, sc. 3 preparing on a whim to banish Bolingbroke, the act that heralds his own downfall:

Draw near,
And list what with our Council we have done.
For that our kingdom's earth should not be soiled
With that dear blood which it hath fostered,
And for our eyes do hate the dire aspect
Of civil wounds ploughed up with neighbour's sword,
And for we think the eagle-winged pride
Of sky-aspiring and ambitious thoughts
With rival-hating envy set on you
To wake our peace, which in our country's cradle
Draws the sweet infant breath of gentle sleep,
Which so roused up with boisterous untuned drums,
With harsh resounding trumpet's dreadful bray
And grating shock of wrathful iron arms,
Might from our quiet confines fright fair peace,
And make us wade even in our kindred's blood,
Therefore we banish you our territories. (I.,3., 123–39)

The syntax of this speech is awkward, the rhythms are all over the place. Four lines begin feebly with the conjunction 'and', a further seven lines begin with prepositions, which have a weakening effect. The syntax reflects Richard's own indecision; unable to come to a clearcut, fair decision, he chooses the worst option of all and stops the tournament to banish the contenders. The hesitancy of the language mirrors the hesitancy and incoherent thoughts of the speaker.

If we compare this scene with Act V, sc. i, the difference is starkly obvious. Richard has been deposed and is being imprisoned, later to be murdered. His wife is being sent back to France, and in a moving scene the two say their final farewells, watched over by Northumberland, who has deserted Richard for Bolingbroke.

King Richard: Northumberland, thou ladder wherewithal
    The mounting Bolingbroke ascends my throne,
    The time shall not be many hours of age
    More than it is, ere foul sin gathering head
    Shall break into corruption. Thou shalt think,
    Though he divide the realm and give thee half,
    It is too little, helping him to all;
    And he shall think that thou, which know'st the way
    To plant unrightful kings, wilt know again,
    Being ne'er so little urg'd, another way
    To pluck him headlong from the usurped throne.

> The love of wicked friends converts to fear;
> That fear to hate, and hate turns one or both
> To worthy danger and deserved death.

Northumberland: My guilt be on my head, and there an end.
Take leave and part; for you must part forthwith.

King Richard: Doubly divorc'd! Bad men, ye violate
A twofold marriage; twixt my crown and me,
And then, betwixt me and my married wife.
Let me unkiss the oath 'twixt thee and me;
And yet, not so, for with a kiss 'twas made.
Part us, Northumberland:I towards the north,
Where shivering cold and sickness pines the clime;
My wife to France; from whence, set forth in pomp,
She came adorned hither like sweet May,
Sent back like Hallowmass or short'st of day.

Queen: And must we be divided? must we part?

King Richard: Ay, hand from hand, my love, and heart from heart.

Queen: Banish us both, and send the king with me.

Northumberland: That were some love but little policy.

Queen: Then whither he goes, thither let me go.

King Richard: So two, together weeping, make one woe.
Weep thou for me in France, I for thee here;
Better far off than near, be ne'er the near.
Go, count thy way with sighs, I mine with groans.

Queen: So longest way shall have the longest moans.

King Richard: Twice for one step I'll groan, the way being short,
And piece the way out with a heavy heart.
Come, come, in wooing sorrow let's be brief,
Since, wedding it, there is such length in grief.
One kiss shall stop our mouths, and dumbly part;
Thus give I mine, and thus take I thy heart.

Queen: Give me mine own again, 'twere no good part
To take on me to keep and kill thy heart.
So, now I have mine own again, be gone,
That I may strive to kill it with a groan.

King Richard: We make woe wanton with this fond delay:
Once more, adieu; the rest let sorrow say.
(ll. 55–102)

This powerful and very moving scene presents Richard as a completely different character from the vacillating ninny of the first act. He is in control of the language, even as he struggles to be in control of his own emotions.

His prophecy of Northumberland's ultimate downfall is tersely argued, and the stychomythic exchange between husband and wife leads through a series of bitter wordgames to the lyricism of the final severance.

The impact of both these scenes is constructed through language, the primary material of the translator. In attempting a translation of a play such as this, instead of worrying about the performance dimension and endeavouring to write 'speakable' or 'performable' lines, the translator needs to look at such scenes independently, as separate units, with their inconsistencies of characterisation and uneasy rhythms. What then happens to those scenes, to that translated text once it is handed over for performance involves a different dynamic and another set of priorities. The task of the translator is to work with the inconsistencies of the text and leave the resolution of those inconsistencies to someone else. Searching for deep structures and trying to render the text 'performable' is not the responsibility of the translator.

The Non-universality of the Subtext

Vicki Ooi has pointed out, with reference to the Chinese theatre, that many non-Western theatres do not have a convention of searching for subtextual patterns within a playtext (Ooi, 1980). The Chinese translator, she suggests, has inherited a dramatic language that is useful for direct, descriptive communication, because the convention of the subtext is completely absent. Referring to a Cantonese translation of Eugene O'Neill's *Long Day's Journey into Night*, she argues that the only strategy open to the translator, given the totally different performance conventions between source and target cultures, is to maintain the 'strangeness' or 'foreignness' of O'Neill's work 'so that the translation must be a discovery to the translator as to his readers'. Ooi stresses the hermeneutic dimension of the translation process here, and this is particularly important when we consider the transfer of playtexts interculturally, in cases where theatre traditions are completely different from one another. Theorists who debate performabilty or speakability or the gestic subtext are invariably discussing European theatre traditions and conventions. Once we move outside Europe, the whole picture changes.

For a start, gestus is culture bound, not universal. Eugenio Barba, through the International School of Theatre Anthropology (ISTA) has demonstrated that there are certain recurrent patterns of physical movement in theatres around the world, phenomena such as the question of balance and equilibrium in representations of the comic and the tragic. But theatres have developed according to very different conventions, and the horizon of expectation of audiences differs radically also. In mainstream

British theatre today, for example, audiences expect a play to run for roughly two and a half hours, with an interval of an additional half an hour: an overall time of three hours. Plays are consequently cut and adapted to that time frame. German audiences have no such expectations; Chinese audiences even less so. This kind of temporal difference is bound to have an effect on translation strategies.

Recognition of theatrical conventions from outside Europe has had an impact on the development of 'multicultural' theatre, a theatre that deliberately rejects acculturation into the target system. In his preface to his translation of the *Mahabharata*, Jean-Claude Carrière explains how he rejected what he saw as a 'normalisation' process, i.e. a deliberate Europeanising of language, and opted not to translate certain words like *dharma* or *kshertrva*, because he recognised the inadequacies of the target language to convey certain ideas (Carrière, 1985). We might also add that this decision not to acculturate also has an ideological dimension, for it assumes that European norms are not universal. But Carrière also warns against the risk of producing an esoteric language for a minority of initiated theatre specialists whose agenda is to keep the 'exotic' theatre object at a distance. In multicultural theatre, differences of language, expectations, performance styles and conventions combine in a new whole, where the audience is actively engaged in the process of decoding and is always denied total understanding. The role of the translator here is to occupy the liminal space between cultures and to facilitate some form of contact between theatre conventions.

Patrice Pavis has talked about the 'crossroads' of cultures, where theatre traditions and practices meet and mingle, and this is a useful image, implying as it does a process of exchange in the encounter between cultural systems (Pavis, 1992). Significantly, the image of the 'crossroads', like the image of the labyrinth, implies a plurality of possibilities and rejects any notion of closure.

Conclusions

From within the labyrinth, or standing at the crossroads, we may assess the situation so far and reflect on ways forward. Firstly, and fundamentally, I believe we need to let go of the old confusion of roles for the translator. The translator cannot hope to do everything alone. Ideally, the translator will collaborate with the members of the team who put a playtext into performance. If such an ideal situation does not happen, then the translator should still not be expected to produce an hypothetical performance text or to second guess what actors might want to do to the translation once they start to work with it.

The time has come for translators to stop hunting for deep structures and coded subtexts. The gestic subtext has been an important methodological approach for many western actors, but it is important to recognise that it is implicitly linked to a theatre of psychological realism. A post-modernist theatre, or a non-European theatre or indeed any form of theatre that is not based on psychological realism has no use for this concept. It belongs to a particular moment in time and to a particular concept of performance and cannot be applied unilaterally as a strategy for theatre translators.

Moreover, there needs to be a recognition of the fact that physical expressivity is not universal and varies from culture to culture. Gesture and body language is represented differently, understood differently, reproduced differently in different contexts and at different time, in accordance with different conventions, different histories and different audience expectations.

What is left for the translator to do is to engage specifically with the signs of the text: to wrestle with the deictic units, the speech rhythms, the pauses and silences, the shifts of tone or of register, the problems of intonation patterns: in short, the linguistic and paralinguistic aspects of the written text that are decodable and reencodable. Some translators may find it helpful to read their translations aloud, but this is hardly performance. Translators of prose and poetry frequently read their work aloud to themselves also, as a way of trying to listen to the flow of their language. We need to go back and develop the work proposed by Veltrusky on the dramatic text as literature. We need to examine more closely the variations in deictic patterns between source and target texts, for example, the role played by intonation patterns or by silence, we need to consider more comprehensively the nature of dialogue text, which, as Rina Ben-Shahar has shown, may be said to constitute a distinct sub-language of its own (Ben-Shahar, 1994).

In terms of Translation Studies, theatre translation has always been the poor relation, and I have tried to suggest that part of the explanation of this lies in the impossible task that has been set for the theatre translator to accomplish. But it is also the case that we know woefully little about the genealogy of theatre translation in comparison with the history of other types of translation, and this needs to be rectified. Translation specialists need to work more closely with theatre historians, and there is a great potential for further research in this neglected area.

References

Sirkku Aaltonen (1996) *Acculturation of the Other. Irish Milieux in Finnish Drama Translation.* Joensuu: Joensuu University Press.

Bassnett, Susan (1978) Translating spatial poetry: An examination of theatre texts in performance. In James Holmes, Jose Lambert and Raymond Van den Broek (eds) *Literature and Translation* (pp. 161–176). Leuven: ACCO.

Bassnett, Susan (1980) The problems of translating theatre texts. *Theatre Quarterly* 10 (38), 47–55.

Bassnett, Susan (1985) Ways through the labyrinth: Strategies and methods for translating theatre texts. In Theo Hermans (ed.) *The Manipulation of Literature* (pp. 87–103). London: Croom Helm.

Bassnett, Susan (1990) Translating for the theatre: Textual complexities. *Essays in Poetics* 15 (1), April, pp. 71–84.

Bassnett, Susan (1991) Translating for the theatre: The case against 'performability'. *TTR* 4 (1), pp. 99–113.

Bassnett, Susan and Hirst, David (1987) *A Woman in Search of Herself* (English version of Luigi Pirandello's *Trovarsi*). BBC Radio 3, 30 June, 1987.

Barba, Eugenio (1985) *Beyond the Floating Islands*. New York: PAH Publications.

Ben-Shahar, Rina (1994) Translating literary dialogue: A problem and its implications for translation into Hebrew. *Target* 6 (2), pp. 195–221.

Carlson, Marvin (1985) Theatrical performance: Illustration, translation, fulfillment or supplement? *Theatre Journal*, March, pp. 5–11.

Carrière, Jean-Claude (1985) Chercher le coeur profond. *Alternatives théâtrales* no. 24.

Frayn, Michael (1989) Christopher Hampton and Timberlake Wertenberger, debate on translation. *Platform Papers* London: Royal National Theatre.

Griffiths, Trevor (transl.) (1978) *The Cherry Orchard. A New English Version*. London: Pluto Press.

Heylen, Romy (1993) *Translation Poetics and the Stage*. London and New York: Routledge.

Kowzan, Tadeusz (1975) *Littérature et spectacle*. The Hague/Paris: Mouton.

Lefevere, André (1992) *Translation, Rewriting and the Manipulation of Literary Fame*. London and New York: Routledge.

Ooi, Vicki (1980) Transcending culture: A Cantonese translation and production of O'Neill's *Long Day's Journey into Night*. In Ortrun Zuber *The Languages of Theatre: Problems in the Translation and Transposition of Drama* (pp. 51–69). London: Pergamon Press.

Pavis, Patrice (1992) *Theatre at the Crossroads of Culture*. Transl. Loren Kruger. London and New York: Routledge.

Pirandello, Luigi (1993) [1908] Illustrators, actors and translators. Transl. Susan Bassnett. In Susan Bassnett and Jennifer Lorch (eds) *Luigi Pirandello in the Theatre. A Documentary Record* (pp. 23–34). Harwood Academic Publishers.

Scolnicov, Hanna and Holland, Peter (eds) (1989) *The Play Out of Context: Transferring Plays from Culture to Culture*. Cambridge: Cambridge University Press.

Tornqvist, Egil (1991) *Transposing Drama*. London: Macmillan.

Ubersfeld, Anne (1978) *Lire le théâtre*. Paris: Editions sociales.

Veltrusky, Jíři (1977) *Drama as Literature* Lisse: The Peter de Ridder Press.

Chapter 7
Acculturating Bertolt Brecht

ANDRÉ LEFEVERE

Writers and their work are translated differently when they are considered 'classics', when their work is recognised as 'cultural capital', and when they are not. Writers become classics, and their work becomes cultural capital not only on their/its own merits, but also because they are rewritten. The present chapter deals with three different types of rewritings of Bertolt Brecht's *Mütter Courage* in English: translations, criticism, and entries in reference works. I hope to show that the three rewritings can be seen to work together, supplementing and contradicting each other, in their efforts to either acculturate Brecht and try to canonise him in English, even to the point of giving him a place among British and American writers including 'Kipling, Swift, Gay, Upton Sinclair, Jack London, Dickens' (Esslin, 1959), or to prevent acculturation and to argue that there is no need to give him a niche in the English canon at all. I hope to illustrate two important general points: one, that the three types of rewriting mentioned above operate in a symbiotic relationship and two, that rewriters, often operating with an agenda of their own, play the most important part in the acculturation and — at least attempted — canonisation of the writers they take an interest in.

Brecht's *Mütter Courage* has been translated into English three times. First by H.R. Hays in 1941, then by Eric Bentley in 1967, and then again by Ralph Manheim in 1972. It is safe to assume that Brecht was relatively unknown in Britain and the US in 1941, even though he had already become a well-known and controversial writer in pre-1933 Germany. Far from canonising him, his native country burnt his books after that year. The Brecht translated in 1967 is the Brecht who had achieved much greater international renown than his younger self in 1941, not least because of the Berliner Ensemble performances of his plays, which had been seen by many British and American theatre people, either in Berlin or during the Berliner Ensemble's tours of European countries and the British Isles, where Brecht achieved his posthumous breakthrough with the 1965 Berliner Ensemble's London production of *The Resistible Rise of Arturo Ui*, when 'British critics began to rave about the precision, the passion, acrobatic prowess, and general excellence of it all' (Esslin, 1969: 83). Finally, the Brecht of 1972 is presented as a classic: Manheim's translation appears in volume five of the *Collected Plays of Bertolt Brecht*, a volume that also contains theoretical writings by Brecht on the theatre in general and on *Mütter Courage* in particular, as well as Charles Laughton's own version of Brecht's *Leben des Galilei*, in addition to Manheim/Willet's translations of *Mother Courage*, the *Life of Galileo*, and the *Trial of Lucullus*.

Hays' translation contains howlers that are unforgivable in any translation of any text. When Mother Courage says, in German: 'Da ist ein ganzes Messbuch dabei, aus Altötting, zum Einschlagen von Gurken' [there is a whole missal there, from Altötting, handy if you want to pickle cucumbers], she says in Hays' English translation: 'There's a whole ledger from Altötting to the storming of Gurken' (B[recht]26/H[ays]5). The prayer book has been transformed into a ledger, presumably because the cucumbers, or 'Gurken' in German, have been transformed into an imaginary town, of the same name, which has been stormed, a translation probably suggested by the 'schlagen' (beat, hit, among other meanings) in the German. If there has, indeed, been something like 'the siege of Gurken', then that siege may well have been the point at which the last transaction was entered into the ledger — a missal would clearly not do in this context. I shall not list Hays' other howlers, except for the one he shares with Bentley. In this case Mother Courage says in German: 'wenn einer nicht hat frei werden wolln, hat der König keinen Spass gekannt' [the king did not treat lightly any attempts to resist being liberated]. Hays makes her say: 'if there had been nobody who needed freeing, the king wouldn't have had any sport' (B58/H25). In Bentley's translation she says: 'if no one had *wanted* to be free, the king wouldn't have had any fun' (B58/B[entley]25).

Hays did not know German all that well, certainly not well enough to catch the slangy and dialect-coloured elements of the language Brecht uses in *Mother Courage*. Bentley's knowledge of German is better, but he still makes the occasional mistake. In both cases, though, the knowledge of German hardly matters. The 1941 *Mother Courage* was not published in book form, but in New Directions' semi-annual anthology of avant garde literature that bears the same name. Since the play was both anti-Nazi and avant garde, nothing much could go wrong. The 1967 *Mother Courage* was published in book form, as part of Bentley's efforts to get Brecht into the American repertoire, efforts that were acknowledged as such at the time: 'a large measure of credit for the wider recognition of Brecht in the United States is due to the drama critic Eric Bentley, who translated several of Brecht's plays and has written several sound critical appreciations of him' (Kunitz 116a). Details were not allowed to stand in the way of the grander design, in both cases. In Manheim and Willet's collected Brecht in English, on the other hand, details match and reinforce the grand design, which has become quite different in the meantime. The collected Brecht intends to make Brecht available to the receiving culture on his own terms. Hays and, especially, Bentley, tried to negotiate as much as possible between the receiving culture and the text about to be received, even on such a basic level as that of language. Bentley, for instance, translates 'Käs aufs Weißbrot' as 'Cheese on pumpernickel' (B23/B3), rather than the more literal 'cheese on bread', probably on the assumption that an American audience would expect Germans to eat their cheese on pumpernickel, since Germany is, after all, where pumpernickel came from. Similarly 'in dem schönen Flandern': [in beautiful Flanders] becomes the much more familiar 'in Flanders' fields' (B52/B22), linking the Thirty Years' War with World War I, as does Bentley's use of 'Kaiser', which he leaves untranslated throughout.

The battle for Brecht, it would seem, has essentially been waged in the fifties and the first half of the sixties, when 'the critical battles' did indeed, in J. Buchanan-Brown's words 'centre around three crucial aspects: his allegiance to the Marxist doctrine, his merit as an artist, the relevance of his postulates for an entirely new direction in the modern theatre' (Cassell's vol. 2 208b). I shall deal with the latter two points first, leaving the doctrinal one for last.

It could be convincingly argued that Brecht the artist was accepted by at least part of the theatre-going audience in England before he was accepted by part of that audience in the USA. The enthusiastic reception of the Berliner Ensemble by a large segment of the British audience in 1956, should also be seen within the context of the debate on whether or not a state subsidised National Theatre ought to be set up in England. The opposition to a National Theatre could 'at last be effectively silenced by pointing to the Berliner Ensemble, led by a great artist, consisting of young, vigorous and anti-establishment actors and actresses, wholly experimental, overflowing with ideas — and state-subsidised to the hilt' (Esslin, 1969: 75–76).

Since part of the theatre establishment in England had a use for Brecht and his theatre, it proceeded to take him under its wing, positively championing his work, especially when 'Kenneth Tynan became drama critic of the London *Observer* in 1954, and very soon made the name of Brecht his trademark, his yardstick of values' (Esslin, 1969: 76). In the US a similar role was played by Eric Bentley, but he did have to tread lightly for a while. His 1951 anthology, *The Play*, does not contain any work by Brecht. Moreover, Bentley states in his introduction to the anthology that 'undue preoccupation with content, with theme, has been characteristic of Marxist critics' (Bentley, 1951: 6). In 1966, on the other hand, Series Three of *From the Modern Repertoire*, edited by Eric Bentley, is 'dedicated to the memory of Bertolt Brecht'.

The very feature that attracts Brecht's champions to his cause, is also the feature that creates the greatest animosity toward him among those who want to work against his acculturation, and that feature is, of course, his very personal view of what the theatre should be, his many 'postulates', which keep circling around various themes, trying to define and/or demonstrate what has come to be known as 'epic theatre'.

A number of strategies have been developed for dealing with the problem of Brecht's 'postulates'.

(1) It is possible to recognise and appreciate the quality of the plays themselves, while dismissing the statements on the theatre out of hand, as in 'the theory of alienation was only so much nonsense, disproved by the sheer theatricality of all his better works' (Gottfried, 1969: 239). In the same vein, Brecht is said to be 'indifferent to dramatic action or plot' (Cassell's 2 208b) and each scene in his plays is said to be 'reminiscent of a talk or a lecture rather than a play' (Cassell's 2 208b).

(2) It is possible to go in for the psychological cop-out, and dismiss Brecht's statements on the theatre as so many instances of a not very successful attempt at rationalising what are, at bottom, irrational factors that would have destroyed him if he had not tried to rationalise them: 'theory does not concern me. I am convinced that Brecht writes as he does, not so much from a predetermined calculation based on what he believes to be the correct goals for the present revolutionary age, as from the dictates of temperament' (Clurman, 1974: 152). This strategy can be taken further and it can be argued that Brecht's temperament was so contradictory that he had to go to the opposite extreme of what he wanted to say in order to be able to say it: 'under the cover of ridicule he could indulge the "high-minded", even religious impulses which his rational, cynical self would not allow him to acknowledge' (Esslin, 1959: 104b).

(3) It is possible to try to show, and it is important to show that you succeed in trying, that Brecht's statements are not really all that new and revolutionary, by rewriting them in terms of older, more traditional concepts of theatre: 'these ideas appear more novel on paper than on the stage, and really they are broadly the principles of comedy, which Brecht applies to plays of more serious content' (Skelton, 1951: 5b). Alternatively, it is possible to acknowledge that Brecht did achieve something, but that the said something was not really worth achieving: 'nobody more effectively than Brecht destroyed the well-made play throughout Europe. But there is a considerable debit side to this

achievement. For one thing, his plays are necessarily unenjoyable' (Pryce-Jones, 1963: 107b).

(4) Finally, and this is perhaps the riskiest, but also potentially the most rewarding strategy, it is possible to convince both theatre people and the public at large that older concepts of theatre are, in fact, able to accommodate Brecht's statements, that there is room for them in one of the theatre's many mansions, and that allowing them to enter into one of those mansions will not make the whole house crumble: 'some critics have interpreted alienation to mean that the audience should be in a constant state of emotional detachment, but in actuality Brecht manipulated aesthetic distance to involve the spectator emotionally and then jar him out of his emphatic response so that he may judge critically what he has experienced' (Brockett, 1971: 216) — a masterful statement indeed, which allows you to have your cake as an Aristotelian and eat it as a Brechtian. Perhaps the ultimate in terms of this strategy has been achieved by Eric Bentley, where he rebaptises 'epic theatre' into the even more technical, but somehow more reassuring sounding 'theatre of Narrative Realism', and goes on to state that this theatre 'has more in common with the great theatre of the remoter past than with the theatre of today and yesterday' (Bentley, 1946: 100b), suggesting that the concept of theatre championed by Brecht's detractors is really the aberration, whereas Brecht is going back to the norms of a more traditional theatre.

The same four strategies surface again in criticism and interpretations of *Mother Courage*, the play, as opposed to Brecht, the writer. The first strategy is illustrated by *Variety*'s review of the 1963 Broadway production: 'sophomorically obvious, cynical, self-consciously drab and tiresome' (quoted in Schieps, 1977: 265). On a more sophisticated level, it is also possible to argue that the play simply doesn't work, because the image of war Brecht gives in it does not correspond to the image of war the critic subscribes to: 'war does make money, which we hold dear; war does create courage, which we admire, war does support the established institutions of society, which we want to maintain, and war does promote a sense of love and brotherhood, which we find valuable' (Corrigan, 1973: 120a).

The second strategy surfaces in *Funk and Wagnall's Guide to World Literature*, and it is important to note that the words are not Clurman's this time. What follows is, rather, Martin Seymour-Smith's reformulation of the strategy: 'His imagination and his own love of life created a work that transcends any thesis... He could not take away Mother Courage's humanity; even rigidly Marxist critics still saw her as human' (642).

John Willet tries the third strategy as early as 1949, in a review of the

Berlin production of *Mütter Courage*, republished in 1984: 'it may be depressing, it may be tiring, but it is never cheap; at worst it is like one of those fat stodgy books which no one wants to read, yet everyone who has read finds satisfying. Such a play is not poured into you in an effortless way, but the effort is worth making' (Willet, 1984: 3b).

Finally, Robert Brustein formulates the fourth strategy as follows: 'Nevertheless, we must also realise that Brecht *does* realise his conscious intentions with the character, and that the tragedy he intentially [*sic*] created coexists with the morality play he designed' (Brustein, 1964: 12a).

Of the three translations under discussion here, Mannheim's is situated between iii and iv. Hays and Bentley weave in and out of ii and iii. The main problem is, of course, to accommodate Brecht's directness of diction and radically new staging to the concept of theatre symbolised by Broadway. In Alan Pryce-Jones' lapidary formulation: 'since they are antibourgeois and antirespectable, they [Brecht's plays] are designed as a threat to the playgoing public rather than a stimulus' (107b/108a). Even the pro-Brecht Willet writes in 1949: 'no audience will be able to get to grips with them [Brecht's plays] if he hems them in with the ugly exotic little cactus edge of his own fads' (4a). For audience, read: American audience. One could just as easily invert the statement and call the Broadway concept of theatre another kind of 'fad'. It is significant that the early Willet, while prepared to accept Brecht on his own terms, still matter of factly accepts Broadway as the norm.

Herbert Blau describes the resistance of Broadway, or rather, the Broadway concept of theatre to Brecht, in a very revealing manner in his account of how a US theatre company actually tackles a production of *Mother Courage*. He starts out by stating the audience's resistance to Brecht as follows: 'we have never driven anybody out of the theatre, as we did occasionally with this play' (Blau, 1964: 7a), and then goes on to explain how the actors tried to overcome a similar reaction. After the first reading through, the actors 'were alienated; they were also bored. The play was static. Only one scene was really moving, that in which the Dumb Daughter Catherine beats her drum on the roof' (7a). The use of the term 'alienated' in this context is strongly reminiscent of the third strategy identified above. It may well describe adequately what the actors felt, but it has nothing whatsoever to do with Brecht's use of the term. Still, the actors keep an open mind, again operating on the level of the third strategy: 'the discovery of this play was, embarrassingly, a measure of our private inadequacies and cultural prejudices' (7b), especially when the actors discover that Brecht's way of staging the play, even though it is very different from what they are used to, actually works in practice: 'how shocked we were at our first dress rehearsal, though we should have known, that our costumes looked like costumes (and should)' (8b). In the end, producing the play makes many actors move from the level of the third strategy to that of the fourth: some of them still keep a 'preference for the latter part of the play; most of us are still prone to recognise as dramatic mainly that which is fast-paced and violent' (9a). But those who have moved from level three to level four recognise that 'drama exists at the calm peripheries of history as much as in its excited middle' (9a), even though one might well ask if this was the kind of realisation Brecht wanted his play to lead to.

To make Brecht fit Broadway, Hays and Bentley try to 'make clear' to their spectators or readers what Brecht wanted his spectators or readers to piece together for themselves. Brecht's stage direction 'Die stumme Kattrin springt vom Wagen und stößt rauhe Laute aus' [the dumb Kattrin jumps from the wagon and emits growling sounds] is rendered by Hays as 'Dumb Kattrin makes a hoarse outcry *because she notices the abduction*' (B37/H12 [italics mine]). Mother Courage's words to Kattrin: 'Du bist selber ein Kreuz: du hast ein gutes Herz' [you're a cross yourself: you have a good heart] are translated by Hays as: 'You're a cross yourself. *What sort of a help to me are you? And all the same* what a good heart you have' (B34/H11), and by Manheim as 'you cross yourself *because* you have a good heart' (B34/M142). What has been italicised is not in the German.

Bentley tries to solve the problem of making Brecht more transparent by means of the excessive use of hyphens and italics: 'Wer seid ihr?' [who are you?] becomes 'Who'd you think *you* are' (B24/B4). 'Aber zu fressen haben wir auch nix' [but we don't have anything to eat either] is turned into: 'A fat lot of difference that makes: we haven't got anything to eat either' (B39/B13). Finally 'der Feldhauptmann wird Ihnen den Kopf abreißen, wenn nix aufm Tisch steht' is rendered as 'I know your problem: if you don't find something to eat and quick, the Chief will-cut-your-fat-head-off' (B40/B14) instead of 'the captain will tear your head off if there's nothing on the table'.

Hays and Bentley also do their best to integrate the songs, which Brecht uses as the 'alienation effect' *par excellence*, fully into the play, approximating the model of the musical. It is interesting to note, in this respect, what happened to the songs in the only Broadway production ever of *Mother Courage*:

> The original text contains nine songs. I have the impression that several of these have been cut — probably because, if they were retained, the time allowed to sing and play them might exceed twenty four minutes and the Musicians' Union would list the production as a 'musical'.

According to regulations, this classification would entail the employment of twenty four musicians at heavy cost. (Clurman, 1966: 62)

Bentley adds 'transitional lines' between the spoken text and the song in 'Das Lied vom Weib und dem Soldaten' [The Song of the Woman and the Soldier], giving the song more of the flavour of the musical: 'To a soldier lad comes an old fishwife/and this old fishwife says she' (B45/B18).

The influence of the musical can also be seen in a tendency toward the vague, the abstract, the cliché in the translation of the songs, as opposed to that of the spoken text. The need to rhyme, moreover, leads to excessive padding, where the original is jarring and concrete, as in: 'Ihr Hauptleut, eure Leut marschieren/Euch ohne Wurst nicht in den Tod/Laßt die Courage sie erst kurieren/Mit Wein von Leib und Geistesnot' [Commanders, your men won't march to their death without sausage. Let Courage heal them first with wine of the pains of body and soul], which Hays translates as: 'Bonebare this land and picked of meat/The fame is yours but where's the bread?/So here I bring you food to eat/And wine to slake and soothe your dread' (B25/H4).

Bentley also makes the texts of the songs conform more to the style and register of the musical. The lapidary, and therefore final:

In einer trüben Früh
Begann mein Qual und Müh
Das Regiment stand im Geviert
Dann ward getrommelt, wies der Brauch
Dann ist der Feind, mein Liebster auch
Aus unsrer Stadt marschiert

[My pain and sorrow began one drab morning. The regiment stood in the square. Then they beat the drums, as is the custom. Then the enemy marched out of our town, my beloved with them]

is padded out with a string of clichés into

The springtime's soft amour
Through summer may endure
But swiftly comes the fall
And winter ends it all.
December came. All of the men
Filed past the trees where once we hid
Then quickly marched away and did
Not come back again (B55/B23).

There is little left of Brecht, but the seasons and the sad reminiscence, so often *de rigueur* on Broadway, are certainly in evidence. The musical takes over completely when Bentley translates 'ein Schnapps, Wirt, sei g'scheit/Ein Reiter hat keine Zeit/Muß für sein Kaiser streiten' [a schnapps, mine host, be quick/A soldier on horseback has no time/he has to fight for his emperor] as 'One schnapps, mine host, be quick, make haste!/A soldier's got no time to waste/He must be shooting, shooting, shooting/His Kaiser's enemies uprooting' (B101/B49). Other refrain lines in the same song are treated with great consistency: 'Er muß gen Mähren reiten' [he must ride to Moravia] becomes 'He must be hating, hating, hating/he cannot keep his Kaiser waiting', while 'Er muß fürn Kaiser sterben' [he has to die for the emperor] becomes 'He must be dying, dying, dying/His Kaiser's greatness glorifying' (B101/B50).

The least that can charitably be said is that Bentley must have believed that this way of translating would make Brecht's acculturation easier than a more literal translation would have done. However, Bentley's translation also makes it easier to imagine the average American actors' adverse reaction, and not to blame them for it.

The terse, episodic structure of Brecht's play and the stage directions designed to give some hint as to the way actors should act are two more features of the epic theatre that do not travel too well into theatres dominated by the well-made play. Hays therefore redivides Brecht's text into acts and scenes. Bentley keeps Brecht's scenes and gives each of them a title, which turns out to be the first line of Brecht's text. Both turn a lapidary stage direction like 'Wenn der Koch kommt, sieht er verdutzt sein Zeug' [when the cook comes, he stares at his things, confused] into something more elaborate, more familiar to a generation of actors brought up on Stanislavsky, or at least the US adaptation of his method: 'Then the Cook returns, still eating. He stares in astonishment at his belongings' and 'A gust of wind. Enter the Cook, still chewing. He sees his things' (B192/H72/B72). Even Manheim does not always trust Brecht on his own: when Kattrin is dead, Mother Courage says: 'Vielleicht schlaft sie' [maybe she's asleep]. The translation reads: 'maybe I can get her to sleep'. Mother Courage then sings the lullaby she also sings in Brecht, and adds: 'Now she's asleep' (B153/M209). The addition is not in the original. Similarly, when Mother Courage decides not to complain to the captain after all, but simply to get up and leave, thereby ending the scene, Bentley adds a stage direction: 'The scrivener looks after her, shaking his head' (B90/B44).

Brecht's dialogue is another problem. It must be made to 'flow' more if it is to fit in with the concept of theatre dominating in Britain and the US. The most obvious strategy to achieve this, is the redistribution of lines. Actors should obviously not be allowed to stand around for too long without anything to say. Consequently, when Yvette, the prostitute, says in the original: 'Dann können wir ja suchen gehn, ich geh gern herum und such mir was aus, ich geh gern mit dir herum, Poldi, das ist doch ein Vergnügen, nicht? Und wenns zwei Wochen dauert?' [Then we can go looking, I love walking about and looking for things, I love walking about with you, Poldi, it's so nice, isn't it? Even if it takes two weeks?] the same passage becomes in Bentley: 'Yvette: Yes, we can certainly look around for something. I love going around looking. I love going around with you, Poldy... The Colonel: Really? Do you? Yvette: Oh, it's lovely. I could take two weeks of it! The Colonel: Really? Could you?' (B76/B36).

In the same vein a little emotion is added where emotion is too patently lacking, at least in Bentley's opinion. Yvette's denunciation of the Cook as 'das ist der schlimmste, wo an der ganzen flandrischen Küste herumgelaufen ist. An jedem Finger eine, die er ins Unglück gebracht hat' [that is the worst guy that ever ran around on the whole Flemish coast. He had one on every finger, and he has ruined them all] becomes: 'he's a bad lot. You won't find a worse on the whole coast of Flanders. He got more girls in trouble than ... (*concentrating on the cook*) Miserable cur! Damnable whore hunter! Inveterate seducer!' (B125/B63). The stage direction and what follows it have been added.

The other 'critical battle' over Brecht concerns his 'allegiance to the Marxist doctrine', when critics tell their readers that Brecht writes the way he writes not 'just for the sake of novelty' (*Twentieth Century Writing*, 1971: 88), but that he tried to subject his audiences 'directly to a Marxist message' (*Twentieth Century Writing*, 1971: 89).

Here again various strategies are deployed. Critics who do not want to acculturate Brecht claim that the attention he attracts has nothing to do with his writing, but that 'a considerable part of his reputation today comes from a cause unconnected with theatre' (Pryce-Jones, 1963: TCLC 1, 108a). Critics who want to acculturate Brecht, on the other hand, need to play down his Marxism in the Cold War atmosphere.

Predictably, one of the most favoured strategies in this respect is, again, that of the psychological cop-out, which basically allows the critic to say that Brecht did not really know what he was doing, and that the viewing and reading audiences should therefore concentrate on his plays, not his ideology: 'his uniqueness as an artist lies not in his content or politics ... but in the manner in which he has translated a bias into drama, production style, and dramatic theory' (Gassner, 1954: 101b). The most that can be said about Brecht's Marxism, within the confines of this strategy, is some throw-away line like 'his Marxism took him on silly sorties into sophomore economics' (O'Donnell, 1969).

It is also possible to recognise Brecht as a great writer, but to deplore the fact that he was a Marxist, rather than to ignore it. To this end, further variants of the cop-out strategy have been developed. One holds that Marxism did not make Brecht happy, in the end: 'the Communist ideology helps him to objectify his feelings and rationalise his art; and it encourages him to attribute an external cause to the cruelty, greed, and lust that he finds in life; but it is never really adequate to Brecht's metaphysical *Angst*' (Brustein, 1990: 111b). No wonder, then, that we are told in the same breath that 'what Brecht really desires is the Buddhist Nirvana' (Brustein, 1990: 112a). In the same vein another critic gives us a glimpse of 'the real Brecht behind the façade of cheerful support for the East German regime; a wistful, disillusioned man, dreaming of the landscape of his childhood in Augsburg' (Esslin, 1959: 119a).

Another variant of this strategy holds that Brecht was grievously punished, indeed, for what he did. Hannah Arendt claims that he lost his 'divine gift' of creativity (114a) 'after he settled down in East Berlin, where he could see, day after day, what it meant to people to live under a Communist regime' (115a). This strategy has the additional advantage of positing the implicit superiority of the West, since it is the West, after all, which has it in its power to absolve Brecht: 'so far it has been the free West which has welcomed this writer, discussed him, learned from him, and performed his plays. Paradoxically, Brecht's survival may depend on the survival of the West which he, by all ordinary standards, had tried so hard to prevent' (Politzer, 1982: 32b).

The supreme irony here is, of course, that the originator of the epic theatre can, himself, be made into a tragic figure, blinded by his own *hamartia*, which keeps him from realising not only that 'he succeeded most with non-Communist audiences who (Brecht believed), misunderstood or missed the social-revolutionary "message" of his plays', but also that 'the damage it [Marxism] did to his work is obvious enough' (Cassell's, 1973: 77b). In its ultimate avatar this strategy even turns Brecht into a Faust-like figure, who sells his soul to Marxism because, in the German Democratic Republic 'he was given what he would never have been given in the West: his own handsomely subsidised theatre' (Cassell's, 1973: 78a).

Another strategy is that of grudging admiration: 'Brecht can be said to be the only writer who wrested from Stalinism anything that is or resembles genuine high art' (Greenberg, 1961: 98a). Similarly, if Brecht was a Marxist, he at least kept his integrity as an artist: 'he never genuflected to communism and as long as he lived he never allowed his theatre to become a shrine' (Corrigan, 1973: 120b).

A final strategy is to pretend that Brecht is not really a Marxist, only superficially so, and that his real commitment transcends any immediate political cause: 'There is a Brecht below the political level ... a poet of democracy in a sense deeper than that applied to the zealous supporters of particular causes' (Bentley, 1953: 98a). How, continuing in the same vein, could Brecht ever really have been a Marxist since 'the modernist view of the irrational is completely incompatible with Marxist thought' (Corrigan, 1973: 120b)?

It should come as no surprise that anything smacking of Marxism, or even remotely of the 'class struggle' vanishes from both Hays' and Bentley's translations. Hays consistently plays down the aggressive pacifism of the original, omitting whole speeches like the bitterly ironic: 'Wie alles Gute ist auch der Krieg am Abfang schwer zu machen. Wenn er dann erst floriert, ist er auch zäh: dann schrecken die Leute zurück vorm Frieden wie die Würfler vorm Aufhören, weil dann müssens zahlen, was sie verloren haben. Aber zuerst schrecken sie zurück vorm Krieg. Er ist ihnen was Neues' [Like all good things, war is not easy in the beginning. But once it gets going, it's hard to get rid of; people become afraid of peace like dice throwers who don't want to stop, because they have to pay up when they do. But they are afraid of war in the beginning. It's new to them].

Hays also weakens the obvious connection between war and commerce in the person of Mother Courage by omitting lines Brecht gives her, such as: 'Und jetzt fahren wir weiter, es ist nicht alle Tage Krieg, ich muß tummeln' [and now let's drive on; there isn't a war on every day. I have to get cracking]. Bentley also goes easy on the pacifism. A statement like 'Man merkts, hier ist zu lang kein Krieg gewesen. Wo soll da Moral herkommen, frag ich? Frieden, das ist nur Schlamperei, erst der Krieg schafft Ordnung. Die Menschheit schießt ins Kraut im Frieden' [You can see there hasn't been a war here for too long. Where do you get your morals from, then, I ask you? Peace is a sloppy business, you need a war to get order. Mankind runs wild in peace] simply becomes 'what they could do with here is a good war' (B22/B3). In addition, certain war-connected words and phrases are put into a nobler register in translation. 'Wir zwei gehn dort ins Feld und tragen die Sach aus unter Männern' [the two of us will go out into that field and settle this business among men] becomes 'the two of us will now go and settle the affair on the field of honor' (B30/B8), and 'mit Spießen und Kanonen' [with spears and guns], is rendered as 'with fire and sword' (B145/B 76). Manheim, who translates later and in a more Brecht-friendly climate, takes the opposite approach and makes the pacifism more explicit, turning 'So macher wollt so maches haben/Was es für manchen gar nicht gab' [so many wanted so much that was not available for many] as 'Some people think they'd like to ride out/The war, leave danger to the brave' (B113/M 185).

Finally, the verdicts some critics render on Brecht around 1972, can easily be correlated with one or more of the strategies mentioned above. Some take the high road, the one that leads beyond Marxism, and write: 'What does Brecht ultimately say? ...Seek always, do not allow yourself to grow rigid at any point and let your goal be the peaceful enjoyment of the goods of life' (Clurman, 1974: 116a). Others damn Brecht because of his Marxism: 'Brecht sided with the would-be jailers of mankind, pretending to be a teacher and liberator of men' (Szczesny, 1969: TCLC 6, 33b). Still others separate the artist from the Marxist, stating that Brecht's plays 'are masterful for their rich variety and satiric, often broadly comic, manner of performing the primary, age-old purpose of drama — to entertain' (Modern World Drama 106b). Others, finally, prefer to remain non-committal, calling Brecht simply 'a major twentieth-century European' (Cassell's, 1973: 77a), conceding merely that he provided 'a much needed tonic for the European theatre as a whole' (Cassell's, 1973: 78b).

I hope to have shown how translation, criticism, and reference works together can create the image of a writer and a work of literature, and I have tried to identify the agenda behind the construction of some of those images. What I have done acquires more importance if we realise that these images of Brecht are the reality of Brecht for many in the viewing and reading audience that cannot understand or read German. For them the image is all there is, and not only in the case of Brecht. All the more reason why we should analyse the ways in which these, and other images are constructed.

References

Bentley, Eric (ed.) (1951) *The Play*. Englewood Cliffs, NJ: Prentice Hall.
Bentley, Eric (1978) [1953] *In Search of Theater*. New York: Atheneum Publishers. Excerpted in *Twentieth Century Literary Criticism* Vol. 1. Eds Dedria Brynofski and Phyllis Carmel Mendelson. Detroit: Gale Research Company.
Bentley, Eric (1978) [1946] *The Playwright as Thinker*. New York: Reynal and Hitchcock. In *Twentieth Century Literary Criticism* Vol. 1. Eds Dedria Brynofski and Phyllis Carmel Mendelson. Detroit: Gale Research Company.
Bentley, Eric (ed.) (1996) *From the Modern Repertoire, Series Three*. Bloomington: Indiana University Press.
Bentley, Eric (ed.) (1967) *Mother Courage*. London: Methuen.
Brecht, Bertolt (1968) *Mütter Courage und Ihre Kinder*. Berlin: Aufbau Verlag.
Brockett, O.G. (1971) *Perspectives on Contemporary Theatre*. Baton Rouge: Louisiana State University Press.
Brustein, Robert (1990) [1964] *The Theatre of Revolt*. New York: Little, Brown, and Co. Excerpted in *Twentieth Century Literary Criticism* Vol. 35. Ed. Paula Kepos. Detroit: Gale Research Company.

Cassell's Encyclopedia of World Literature (1973). New York: William Morrow.

Clurman, Harold (1966) *The Naked Image*. New York: Macmillan.

Clurman, Harold (1974) Bertolt Brecht. In M. Freedman (ed.) *Essays in the Modern Drama*. Boston: Heath.

The Concise Encyclopedia of Modern World Literature (1963). New York: Hawthorn Books.

Corrigan, Robert W. (1978) [1973] *The Theatre in Search of a Fix*. New York: Delacorte Press. In *Twentieth Century Literary Criticism* Vol. 1. Eds Dedria Brynofski and Phyllis Carmel Mendelson. Detroit: Gale Research Company.

Esslin, Martin (1978) [1959] *Brecht: The Man and His Work*. New York: Doubleday. In *Twentieth Century Literary Criticism* Vol. 1. Eds Dedria Brynofski and Phyllis Carmel Mendelson. Detroit: Gale Research Company.

Esslin, Martin (1969) *Reflections*. Garden City, NY: Doubleday.

Funk and Wagnall's Guide to World Literature (1973). New York: Funk and Wagnall.

Gassner, John (1978) [1954] *The Theatre in Our Times*. New York: Crown Publishers. In *Twentieth Century Literary Criticism* Vol. 1. Eds Dedria Brynofski and Phyllis Carmel Mendelson. Detroit: Gale Research Company.

Gottfried, M. (1969) *Opening Nights*. New York: Putnam.

Greenberg, Clement (1978) [1961] *Art and Culture*. Boston: Beacon Press. In *Twentieth Century Literary Criticism* Vol. 1. Eds Dedria Brynofski and Phyllis Carmel Mendelson. Detroit: Gale Research Company.

Hays, H.R. (1941) *Mother Courage*. New York: New Directions.

Manheim, Ralph (1972) Mother Courage. In Ralph Manheim and John Willet (eds) *Brecht. Collected Plays* Vol. 5. New York: Vintage Books.

Modern World Drama (1972). New York: Dutton.

O'Donnell, J.P. (1978) [1969] The Ghost of Brecht. *The Atlantic Monthly*, January 1969. In *Twentieth Century Literary Criticism* Vol. 1. Eds Dedria Brynofski and Phyllis Carmel Mendelson. Detroit: Gale Research Company.

Politzer, Heinz (1982) How epic is Bertolt Brecht's epic theater? *Modern Language Quarterly*. Excerpted in Sharon K. Hall (ed.) *Twentieth Century Literary Criticism* Vol. 6. Detroit: Gale Research Company.

Pryce-Jones, Alan (1978) [1963] Brecht. *Theatre Arts*, June 1963. In *Twentieth Century Literary Criticism* Vol. 1. Eds Dedria Brynofski and Phyllis Carmel Mendelson. Detroit: Gale Research Company.

Schieps, K.H. (1977) *Bertolt Brecht*. New York: Putnam.

Skelton, Geoffrey (1990) [1951] Bertolt Brecht's Mother Courage. *World Review*, No. 23, January. In *Twentieth Century Literary Criticism* Vol. 35. Ed. Paula Kepos. Detroit: Gale Research Company.

Szczesny, Gerhard (1969) *The Case Against Bertolt Brecht*. New York: Ungar, 1969. In *Twentieth Century Literary Criticism* Vol. 6.

Twentieth Century Authors. First Supplement (1965). New York: Wilson.

Twentieth Century Writing (1971). Levittown, NY: Transatlantic Arts.

Willet, John (1990) [1984] *Brecht in Context*. London: Methuen. In *Twentieth Century Literary Criticism* Vol. 35. Ed. Paula Kepos. Detroit: Gale Research Company.

Chapter 8

The Translation Turn in Cultural Studies

SUSAN BASSNETT

In 1990, André Lefevere and I edited a collection of essays entitled *Translation, History and Culture*. We co-wrote the introductory essay to the volume, intending it as a kind of manifesto of what we saw as a major change of emphasis in translation studies. We were trying to argue that the study of the practice of translation had moved on from its formalist phase and was beginning to consider broader issues of context, history and convention:

> Once upon a time, the questions that were always being asked were 'How can translation be taught?' and 'How can translation be studied?' Those who regarded themselves as translators were often contemptuous of any attempts to teach translation, whilst those who claimed to teach often did not translate, and so had to resort to the old evaluative method of setting one translation alongside another and examining both in a formalist vacuum. Now, the questions have changed. The object of study has been redefined; what is studied is the text embedded in its network of both source and target cultural signs and in this way Translation Studies has been able both to utilize the linguistic approach and to move out beyond it. (Bassnett & Lefevere, 1990)

We called this shift of emphasis 'the cultural turn' in translation studies, and suggested that a study of the processes of translation combined with the praxis of translating could offer a way of understanding how complex manipulative textual processes take place: how a text is selected for translation, for example, what role the translator plays in that selection, what role an editor, publisher or patron plays, what criteria determine the strategies that will be employed by the translator, how a text might be received in the target system. For a translation always takes place in a continuum, never in a void, and there are all kinds of textual and extratextual constraints upon the translator. These constraints, or manipulatory processes involved in the transfer of texts have become the primary

123

focus of work in translation studies, and in order to study those processes, translation studies has changed its course and has become both broader and deeper.

In the 1970s, anyone working in translation studies experienced a clear demarcation line between that work and other types of literary or linguistic research. The study of translation occupied a minor corner of applied linguistics, an even more minor corner of literary studies, and no position at all in the newly developing cultural studies. Even those who worked in translation and other related fields appeared to experience a kind of schizophrenic transformation when it came to methodological questions. In an age that was witnessing the emergence of deconstruction, people still talked about 'definitive' translations, about 'accuracy' and 'faithfulness' and 'equivalence' between linguistic and literary systems. Translation was the Cinderella subject, not taken seriously at all, and the language used to discuss work in translation was astonishingly antiquated when set against the new critical vocabularies that were dominating literary studies in general. To pass from a seminar on literary theory to a seminar on translation in those days was to move from the end of the twentieth century to the 1930s. Debate on translation was dominated by evaluative critical language.

The first clear signal of a change in the wind was, I believe, the Leuven seminar of 1976, which brought together for the first time scholars from Israel working on polysystems theory with scholars in the Low Countries and a handful of people from elsewhere in Europe. There André Lefevere was given the task of drawing up a definition of translation studies, which appeared in the 1978 proceedings. The goal of the discipline (he saw it *as* a discipline at that stage) was to 'produce a comprehensive theory which can be used as a guideline for the production of translations'. The theory was to be neither neopositivistic, nor hermeneutic in inspiration and should be constantly tested against case-studies. Instead, It would be dynamic, not static because it would be in a state of continuous evolution. The statement went on to add:

> It is not inconceivable that a theory elaborated in this way might be of help in the formulation of literary and linguistic theory; just as it is not inconceivable that translations made according to the guidelines tentatively laid down in the theory might influence the development of the receiving culture. (Lefevere, 1978)

So theory and practice were to be indissolubly intertwined; theory was not to exist in the abstract, it was to be dynamic and involved a study of the specifics of translation practice. Theory and practice were to supply mutual nourishment.

This very brief statement by Lefevere, which Edwin Gentzler has described as 'a fairly modest proposal' (Gentzler, 1993) nevertheless laid down some ground rules for the next stage in developing translation studies. Fundamental to the statement was a rejection of the old evaluative position, and a refusal to locate translation studies either strictly within literary studies or in linguistics. This, with hindsight, we can see as crucially important: what was effectively being proposed, though none of the proposers realised it at the time, was for translation studies to occupy a new space of its own.

What we can also see, looking back, is that already translation studies shared common ground with that other rapidly developing interdisciplinary field, cultural studies. From its origins as a counter-hegemonic movement within literary studies, challenging the dominance of a single concept of 'Culture' determined by a minority, the subject had moved by the late 1970s, shifting ground away from literature towards sociology. Richard Johnson, one of the pioneers of the subject, warned against the dangers of splitting the sociological from the literary within cultural studies, pointing out that:

> Cultural processes do not correspond to the contours of academic knowledges as they stand. Cultural studies must be interdisciplinary or a-disciplinary in its tendency. Each approach tells us about one small aspect of a larger process. Each approach is theoretically partisan, but also very partial in its objects. (Johnson, 1986)

Cultural studies, Johnson, says must be 'interdisciplinary' or 'a-disciplinary', which is what the Leuven group were effectively saying about translation studies back in 1976. With such similar agendas, it is hardly surprising that the meeting between cultural studies and translation studies, when it finally happened, would be a productive one. Work in both fields called into question disciplinary boundaries and seemed to be moving towards the notion of a new space in which interaction could happen. No single approach would be prioritised, and the partisan nature of different approaches was established from the outset.

The Leuven group did, however, in the early years, tend to favour one particular approach. From 1970 onwards, Itamar Even-Zohar, the Israeli literary theorist, had been propounding his polysystems approach to the study of literatures. He was explicit about the source of his theories: they derived from the Russian formalists. The pioneering work of Tynjanov, Eichenbaum or Zirmunski on literary historiography and history, claimed

Even-Zohar, had never been fully appreciated or developed. There was minimal research in literary studies into the historical functions of a text, not only translated texts but also children's literature, detective fiction, romantic fiction and a host of other genres. Here again, we can see the close parallels between translation studies and cultural studies: both questioned the distinction made within traditional criticism between 'high' and 'low' culture; both mounted a challenge to the concept of the literary canon; both urged a broadening of the study of literature to include the functions of a text in a given context. Following Bahktin and Lotman, Even-Zohar argued that the mechanism of relations between what he called 'high' and 'low' literature (the terminology that would be seriously challenged by cultural studies) needed proper investigation. Any study of literature that ignored works deemed to have no artistic merit was bound to be flawed and would result in a completely inadequate picture of textual production and reception.

Even-Zohar's contribution to the 1976 Leuven seminar was a paper entitled 'The position of Translated Literature within the Literary Polysystem', which remains a seminal text for scholars of translation studies. Even-Zohar proposed, by applying his systemic notion of literary study to translation, a new way of looking at translation. Questions needed to be asked about the correlations between translated works and the target system, about why certain texts might be selected for translation at a given time and others ignored and then about how the translations might adopt specific norms and behaviours. Why, for example, we might ask, did Fitzgerald's Rubaiyat of Omar Khayham enter into the English literary system so completely that it has ceased to be regarded as a translation, when other 19th century translations of similar texts disappeared without trace? The old aesthetic argument plainly does not hold here; other factors must have been in play, and it is an investigation of those factors that should occupy the translation studies scholar.

Even-Zohar also raised other significant questions: what might the dynamics be in a literary system between innovation and conservatism, and what role might translated literature have to play here. He went on to suggest that there might be a whole other way of looking at the role of translation in literature, seeing translation as a major shaping force for change. This notion of translation as a crucial instrument of literary renewal was a very radical one, and one which traditional literary history had tended to downplay.

We might take as an example the case of European lyric poetry. A classic comparative study of the field is Peter Dronke's *The Medieval Lyric*, a very erudite and immensely readable book that traces the development of the lyric across medieval Europe, following the *'chansonniers* or *Liederhand-scriften* in all their diversity' (Dronke, 1968). Dronke discusses the fusion of Roman and Christian traditions, and the similarities and differences between religious and secular lyric verse. A central chapter is entitled 'The Transformations of the Medieval Love Lyric', and looks at how the Provençal lyric entered Italian and was transformed into the *dolce stil nuovo*. Missing from Dronke's analysis is adequate discussion of the links between the early Provençal and Catalan lyric and Arabic poetry, but others have taken that task in hand. What is striking about Dronke's study, however, is that at no point does he ever discuss the role played by translation in the development and dissemination of the lyric. Yet unless we assume that all singers and poets were multilingual, then obviously translation was involved, as a fundamental activity.

A translation studies approach to the medieval lyric would use a similar comparative methodology to Dronke's, but would ask different questions. It would also look at the development of a literary form in terms of changing sociological patterns across Europe (the end of feudalism, the rise of the city state etc.) and in terms of the history of language. For the development of vernacular languages in Europe was bound up with translation, just as several centuries later, in the Renaissance, the rise of vernacular languages to a status equal to that of the classical languages was also accompanied by a ferment of translation activity. Far from being a marginal enterprise, translation was at the core of the processes of transformation of literary forms and intimately connected to the emergence of national vernaculars.

Even-Zohar proposed the systematic study of the conditions that enable translation to take place in a given culture. In a controversially worded statement, he argued that there are certain conditions that can be discerned whenever major translation activity takes place:

> (a) when a polysystem has not yet been crystallised; i.e. when a literature is 'young', in the process of being established; (b) when a literature is either 'peripheral' or 'weak', or both, and (c) when there are turning points, crises or literary vacuums. (Even-Zohar, 1978a)

Today, we find this statement somewhat crude. What does it mean to define a literature as 'peripheral' or 'weak'? These are evaluative terms and present all kinds of problems. Is Finland 'weak', for example, or Italy, since they both translate so much? In contrast, is the United Kingdom 'strong' and 'central' because it translates so little? Are these criteria literary or political? This is the same difficulty encountered by scholars working with the terminology of 'minority/majority', of course. But despite its crudity, it is still startlingly important, for it can be opened out into a call for a radical rethinking of how we draw up literary histories, how we map out the shaping forces of the past and present.

Polysystems theory opened so many avenues to researchers in translation studies that it is hardly surprising that it dominated thinking for the next decade. All kinds of new work began to be undertaken: the systematic study of the history of translation and translating, the recovery of the statements by translators and translation theory of previous times. This kind of work paralleled similar research in women's studies, particularly of the 'hidden from history' variety.

There was a great deal of valuable, essentially descriptive research, and a great deal of comparative study that followed James Holmes' model of mapping out hierarchies of correspondences between texts in order to better analyse translators' strategies (Holmes, 1988).

There was also some criticism of the polysystems approach, most notably that it had shifted attention too far away from the source text and context onto the target system. This was inevitable. Part of the brief of early polysystems thinking was to get away from notions of a dominant literary canon, and by emphasising the fortunes of a text in its target context, problems of the status of the source text could be set to one side. But as research expanded, so translation scholars began to investigate previously marginalised areas. In similar fashion, early work in cultural studies tended to be contestatory and oppositional, setting itself firmly against the concept of studying canonical texts and arguing for a broader literary spectrum that encompassed (and indeed emphasised) the popular.

By the late 1980s, a lot was happening in translation studies, and a great deal of activity was taking place outside Europe. For polysystems theory, useful though it was to start us all thinking in new ways about cultural history, was a European product. But the work in Canada, in India, in Brazil and Latin America that was looking in very complex ways at ideological issues surrounding translation did not use polysystems theory as a starting point. The concerns of Latin America involved the relationship between source and target extended to a discussion of the relationship between colonised and coloniser. In his essay on the Brazilian anthropophagist movement, 'Tupy or not Tupy: Cannibalism and Nationalism in Contemporary Brazilian Literature', Randall Johnson discusses the metaphor of cannibalism as a statement of cultural identity:

> Metaphorically speaking, it represents a new attitude towards cultural relationships with hegemonic powers. Imitation and influence in the traditional sense of the word are no longer possible. The *antropofagos* do not want to copy European culture, but rather to devour it, taking advantage of its positive aspects, rejecting the negative and creating an

> original national culture that would be a source of artistic expression rather than a receptacle for forms of cultural expression elaborated elsewhere. (Johnson, 1987)

There is no space here to go into the intricacies of the cannibalistic argument, but it is important because it provides us with a clear post colonial metaphor that can be applied to the history of literary transfer and to the history of translation. Traditional notions of translation saw it essentially as a 'copy' of an 'original'. Today, we can see that such terminology is ideologically loaded, and we can also see that it developed at a certain point in time. But significantly, the colony has so often been regarded as the 'copy' of the 'home-country', the original. Any challenge to that notion of original and copy, with the implications of status that go with it, is effectively a challenge to a Eurocentric world view. The antropofagos offered the metaphor of cannibalisation, the ritual devouring that would be in the control of the devourer, the colonised rethinking the relationship with the original coloniser. This is clearly a post colonial perspective.

So also is the perspective on translation offered by Sherry Simon when she argues that:

> The poetics of translation belongs to a realization of an aesthetics of cultural pluralism. The literary object is fragmented, in a manner analogous to the contemporary social body. (Simon, 1996a)

The key phrase here is 'cultural pluralism'. The post-colonial perspective throws into crisis any notion of fixed boundaries and frontiers become unstable. We are compelled to recognise what Tejaswini Niranjana has defined as the strategies of containment that translation produces. For, she argues, 'translation reinforces hegemonic versions of the colonised, helping them acquire what Edward Said calls representations or objects without history' (Niranjana, 1992).

Now wait a minute, someone may say. Didn't a whole line of thinking in translation emerge out of the cultural work of Bible translators like Eugene Nida? Yes, of course it did; but Nida's assumptions about culture derived from anthropology, and we hardly need reminding of the Eurocentric bias of anthropology until very recently. Moreover, Nida's translation work, splendid though it is, comes out of a specific purpose: the translation of a Christian text with the goal of converting non-Christians to a different spiritual viewpoint. His *Customs and Cultures* is subtitled: 'Anthropology for Christian Missions', and the opening sentence of the volume reads: 'Good missionaries have always been good anthropologists' (Nida, 1954).

In case anyone fails to recognise the ideological assumptions underpinning much thinking on anthropology, let us consider the famous (or infamous) case of Wole Soyinka, who in his *Myth, Literature and the African World* recounts his attempt in the early 1970s to offer series of lectures on African literature at Cambridge, when he was Visting Fellow. He was not permitted to give the lectures in the English department and eventually a space was found for him in the Department of Social Anthropology. The English department, he notes, 'did not believe in any such beast as African literature' (Soyinka, 1976). For many Europeans, any non-European cultures were automatically 'anthropologised' and their cultures studied and evaluated as 'other'. The norm was European.

I am not attacking cultural anthropology outright. There are many viewpoints in anthropology, and indeed cultural anthropology and now translation studies have also been moving more closely together. What I want to do is simply to posit the notion that the terms of reference of early 'culturalists' in translation studies derived from a Eurocentric anthropological perspective and not from a cultural studies perspective. That was to come later.

Let us now turn to look at the evolution of cultural studies. The field of study is generally held to have begun in the 1960s, initiated by the publication of a series of texts by British academics who had worked in universities and in adult education. Richard Hoggart's *The Uses of Literacy* appeared in 1957, followed by Raymond Williams' *Culture and Society* and by E.P. Thompson's *The Making of the English Working Class* in 1963. Hoggart set up the Centre for Contemporary Cultural Studies at the University of Birmingham in 1964 and the rest, we might say, is history.

The work of Hoggart, Williams and Thompson did not constitute any kind of school or locus of strategic thinking when their books first appeared. It was only later that they came to be seen as a coherent group, because of their common concern with aspects of the English class system and their commitment to reassessing the meaning of the term 'culture'. Their starting point in the post-war period was the recognition of a gap in intellectual life in Britain: there was no broad notion of culture that could cut across regional and class lines. Raymond Williams in particular challenged the way in which F.R. Leavis had used 'culture', to describe exclusively high cultural forms. Williams argued that no account of 'culture' can ignore the popular culture that is the expression of working class life. In *Culture and Society*, he suggested that the world was now so complex that no individual could lay claim to total understanding and participation, and hence no single perspective could or should be prioritised:

> any predictable civilization will depend on a wide variety of highly specialized skills, which will involve, over definite parts of a culture, a

fragmentation of experience … A culture in common, in our own day, will not be the simple all-in-all society of old dream. It will be a very complex organization, requiring continual adjustment and redrawing …To any individual, however gifted, full participation will be impossible, for the culture will be too complex. (Williams, 1957)

Williams posits here the notion of a complex culture that can never be grasped in its entirely and will always be fragmented, partly unknown and partly unrealised. Like Hoggart, he saw culture as plurivocal and as process, a shifting mass of signs rather than a single entity. In the early years of cultural studies, as the subject sought to establish itself within the academy, the principle concern was to reevaluate oral culture and working class culture, to reclaim the word 'culture' for a mass public rather than an elite minority. Under the leadership of Hoggart's successor, Stuart Hall, the Birmingham Centre moved to considerations of race and gender also, and became less specifically English, drawing more upon theoretical work from the continent of Europe.

Anthony Easthope has long argued that the move from literary studies to cultural studies is an inevitable, ongoing process. In a recent essay, entitled 'But what *is* cultural studies?', he traces the transformations that cultural studies has undergone since the late 1950s and argues that there have been effectively three phases: what he calls the Culturalist phase of the 1960s, the Structuralist phase of the 1970s and the Post-structuralist/ Cultural Materialist phase of the last twenty years (Easthope, 1997). These three phases correspond to different stages in the establishment of the subject as an academic discipline. The culturalist phase records the period when the principal challenge was to the appropriation of the term 'culture' by an elite minority, and the goal was to broaden concepts of 'culture' to include other than canonical texts. The structuralist phase marks the period when attention shifted to an investigation of the relationship between textuality and hegemony, and the third stage reflects the recognition of cultural pluralism.

This tripartite distinction, which traces in broad brush strokes a series of profoundly significant shifts of emphasis that have affected the study of literature just as much as the study of culture, could just as well apply to translation studies over the last twenty years or so. In translation studies, the culturalist phase would describe the work of Nida and probably also of Peter Newmark, as well as the work of scholars such as Catford or Georges Mounin. The value of their attempts to think culturally, to explore the problem of how to define equivalence, to wrestle with notions of linguistic versus cultural untranslatability is undeniable. The problem that the next wave of translation scholars had with that early work was that it was so pragmatic and unsystematic, and it was also unconcerned with history.

The polysystems phase may also be described as a structuralist phase, for systems and structures dominated thinking in the field for a time. We may have used figurative language and talked about 'mapping' (Holmes) labyrinths (Bassnett) or even refractions (Lefevere) but what we were concerned with was a more systematic approach to the study and practice of translation. While translation studies took on polysystems theory, cultural studies delved more deeply into gender theory and the study of youth cultures. It also began to move away from the specifically English focus, and in the 1980s cultural studies expanded rapidly in many parts of the world, notably in the United States and Canada and Australia, changing and adapting as it moved. Questions of cultural identity, multiculturalism, linguistic pluralism became part of the agenda, shifting the emphasis away from those specifically British concerns of the early years. What has remained of cultural studies in the British context, however, can be described as cultural materialism, which Alan Sinfield has defined as a homegrown British alternative to the American new historicism (Dollimore & Sinfield, 1985).

In an essay entitled 'Shifting Boundaries, Lines of Descent', Will Straw endeavours to summarise what has happened to cultural studies in the United States. Cultural studies, he claims, 'represented the turn within a number of disciplines in the humanities' to concerns and methods that had previously been seen as sociological:

> towards, for example, the ethnography of audiences in media studies, the study of intellectual formations and institutional power in literary history, or accounts of the construction of social space in a variety of cultural forms. (Straw, 1993)

And he also points out that cultural studies offered a way forward for English studies and film studies that had, as he puts it, 'lived through their post-structuralist moments'. I take this to mean that they had become enmeshed in a post-structuralist discourse as limiting as old formalism had been, and in consequence unable to deal with the vital new ways of thinking about textual practices that were becoming so evident in the rest of the world.

So cultural studies in its new internationalist phase turned to sociology, to ethnography and to history. And likewise, translation studies turned to ethnography and history and sociology to deepen the methods of analysing what happens to texts in the process of what we might call 'intercultural transfer', or translation. The moment for the meeting of cultural studies and translation studies came at exactly the right time for both. For the great debate of the 1990s is the relationship between globalisation, on the one hand, between the increasing interconnectedness of the world-system in commercial, political and communication terms and the rise of nationalisms on the other. Globalisation is a process, certainly: but there is also massive resistance to globalisation. As Stuart Hall points out, identity is about defining oneself against what one is not:

> To be English is to know yourself in relation to the French, and the hot-blooded Mediterraneans, and the passionate traumatized Russian soul. You go round the entire globe: when you know what everybody else is, then you are what they are not. (Hall, 1991)

In short, cultural studies has moved from its very English beginnings towards increased internationalisation, and has discovered the comparative dimension necessary for what we might call 'intercultural analysis'. Translation studies has moved away from an anthropological notion of culture (albeit a very fuzzy version) and towards a notion of cultures in the plural. In terms of methodology, cultural studies has abandoned its evangelical phase as an oppositional force to traditional literary studies and is looking more closely at questions of hegemonic relations in text production. Similarly, translation studies has moved on from endless debates about 'equivalence' to discussion of the factors involved in text production across linguistic boundaries. The processes that both these interdisciplinary fields have been passing through over the past two or three decades have been remarkably similar, and have led in the same direction, towards a greater awareness of the international context and the need to balance local with global discourses. Methodologically, both have used semiotics to explore the problematics of encoding and decoding.

The often uneasy relationship between literary studies and sociology that has characterised debates in cultural studies also has its parallel in translation studies in the uneasy relationship between literary studies and linguistics. But here again, there have been significant changes. Linguistics has also undergone its own cultural turn, and a great deal of work currently taking place within the broad field of linguistics is of immense value to translation: research in lexicography, in corpus linguistics and frame analysis demonstrate the importance of context and reflects a broader cultural approach than the old-style contrastive linguistics of the past.

A fundamental line of debate within cultural studies has focused upon the notion of value — whether aesthetic value or material value — as culturally determined. The old idea was that texts had some kind of intrinsic universal value of their own that helped them to survive down the ages. So

Homer, for example, or Shakespeare were presented as monolithic universal writers. The idea of a literary canon is premised upon the universal greatness of key writers, whose works transcend time and offer, as Leavis puts it, 'the finest human experience of the past' (Leavis, 1930). But as cultural studies developed, so the question of the conscious construction of aesthetic ideals acquired significance. Alongside our admiration for Shakespeare, questions need to be asked about how we know what we do know about Shakespeare and his plays and to what extent other factors than purely aesthetic criteria come into play. These questions are also asked within translation studies, where it is apparent that the transfer of texts across cultures by no means depends on the supposed intrinsic value of the text itself alone.

If we were to consider both Homer and Shakespeare from another angle than that of their literary stature, either from within cultural studies or translation studies, all kinds of questions would arise. In the case of Homer, we might need to ask how ancient texts have been handed down to us, how representative they might be, given that obviously far more texts have been lost than we have to hand at the present time, how they might have been read originally and by whom, how commissioned and paid for, what purpose they might have served in their original context. Beyond this archaeological survey, we would then need to consider the history of the fortunes of Homer in western literatures, paying especial attention to the rediscovery of the world of the ancient Greeks in the Enlightenment and the use of Greek models in education in the nineteenth century. We would also need to look at the history of translations of Homer, and the role played by those translations in different literary systems. Perhaps most significantly today, as the learning of ancient Greek declines, we would need to consider why Homer continues to occupy such a significant position in the literary hierarchy when almost nobody has access to any of his writings. Except through translation, of course.

Similarly with Shakespeare, we would need to consider the complex method of production of the plays in the first place (whether written prior to rehearsals with actors, during rehearsals and transcribed by someone, or written piecemeal as roles for individual actors to modify themselves, similar to the scenarii of the commedia dell'arte), the sources employed in that process of production, the even more complex history of the editing of the plays, the fortunes of Shakespeare prior to the eighteenth century, the great Shakespeare boom of early Romanticism, and the gradual process of canonisation that has taken place ever since. We would also need to look at the very different Shakespeares that appear in different cultures: the radical, political author of Central and Eastern Europe, for example, or the high priest of the imperial British ideal who was exported to India and the colonies. And in considering how these different Shakespeares have been created, we are led back to the role played by translation.

Both translation studies and cultural studies are concerned primarily with questions of power relations and textual production. The idea that texts might exist outside a network of power relations is becoming increasingly difficult to accept, as we learn more about the shaping forces that control the world in which we live and about those forces that controlled the world in which our predecessors lived. Before he died, André Lefevere was working out a theory of cultural grids, based on the work of Pierre Bourdieu and his ideas of cultural capital. In Lefevere's schema, a kind of grid system can be mapped out that shows the role and place of texts within a culture and the role they might occupy in another culture. Such a system would show clearly that texts undergo all kinds of variations in status both intertemporally and interculturally, and would help us to explain some of the vagaries of those changes in terms other than those of greater or lesser aesthetic value.

As any translation studies scholar knows, a comparison of translations of the same text, particularly of a text that has been translated frequently, exposes the fallacy of universal greatness. The translations that are heralded as definitive at one moment in time can vanish without trace a few years later. Exactly the same happens with all types of text, but we are less clearly able to see the process than with translations of the same text. Countless hugely successful authors have disappeared completely, and it takes a concerted effort, such as the deliberate policy of rediscovering women authors undertaken by feminist scholarship, for example, to excavate those lost texts. As Sherry Simon succinctly puts it:

> Those spaces which were identified as universal (the great humanist tradition, the canon of great books, the public space associated with democratic communication, the model of culture which sustained the ideal of citizenship) have been exposed as being essentially expressive of the values of the white, European and middle-class male. (Simon, 1996b)

So far, the links between cultural studies and translation studies have remained tenuous. A great deal of work in cultural studies, particularly in the English-speaking world, has been monolingually based, and attention has been focused on the investigation of cultural policies and practices from the inside. Increasingly, however, there is a move towards intercultural studies, and this is already well-established within, for example, gender studies, film studies or media studies. On the whole though, while the translation studies world has been slow to use methods developed within cultural studies, the cultural studies world has been even slower in recognising the value of research in the field of translation. Yet the parallels between these two important interdisciplinary fields and the overlap between them are so significant that they can no longer be ignored. The cultural turn in translation studies happened more than a decade ago; the translation turn in cultural studies is now well underway.

Both cultural studies and translation studies practitioners recognise the importance of understanding the manipulatory processes that are involved in textual production. A writer does not just write in a vacuum: he or she is the product of a particular culture, of a particular moment in time, and the writing reflects those factors such as race, gender, age, class, and birthplace as well as the stylistic, idiosyncratic features of the individual. Moreover, the material conditions in which the text is produced, sold, marketed and read also have a crucial role to play. Bourdieu points out that:

> every power which manages to impose meanings and to impose them as legitimate by concealing the power relations which are the basis of its force, adds its own symbolic force to those power relations. (Bourdieu & Passeron, 1977)

Translation, of course, is a primary method of imposing meaning while concealing the power relations that lie behind the production of that meaning. If we take censorship as an example, then it is easy to see how translation can impose censorship while simultaneously purporting to be a free and open rendering of the source text. By comparing the translated version with the original, the evidence of such censorship is easy to see where written texts are concerned. The novels of Emile Zola, for example, were heavily cut and edited by translators and publishers when they first appeared in English. Recently a number of researchers have begun to look at other, less immediately identifiable forms of censorship, particularly in cinema, where, for example, technical factors can be used as means of removing material deemed unacceptable (the particular constraints of sub-titling, for example, with the restricted number of characters that can appear in a single line, or the need in dubbing to make sounds match physical movements shown on screen). It is also interesting to speculate on whether the development of dubbing industries in certain countries is related to the existence at different points in time of totalitarian governments. Why do Italy, Germany, Greece, Spain, the former Soviet Union, China and numerous other countries that have endured dictatorships or military regimes have established dubbing industries as opposed to the use of subtitles? For dubbing erases the original voices, and restricts access to other languages. Subtitling, in contrast, makes a comparative perspective possible, as audiences are allowed to access both source and target systems.

Lawrence Venuti points out that translation, wherever, whenever and however it takes place, is always to some extent circumscribed:

> Every step in the translation process — from the selectionof foreign texts to the implementation of translation strategies to the editing, reviewing and reading of translations — is mediated by the diverse cultural values that circulate in the target language, always in some hierarchical order. (Venuti, 1995)

Translation is therefore always enmeshed in a set of power relations that exist in both the source and target contexts. The problems of decoding a text for a translator involve so much more than language, despite the fact that the basis of any written text *is* its language. Moreover, the importance of understanding what happens in the translation process lies at the heart of our understanding of the world we inhabit. And if translation studies has been increasingly concerned with the relationship between individual texts and the wider cultural system within which those texts are produced and read, it is therefore not surprising that within cultural studies, and in post-colonial theory in particular, translation is increasingly being seen both as actual practice and as metaphor.

Homi Bhabha, in an essay entitled 'How Newness Enters the World', rereads Walter Benjamin and considers the role of translation in cultural (re)negotiation:

> Translation is the performative nature of cultural communication. It is language *in actu* (enunciation, positionality) rather than language *in situ* (*enoncé* or propositionality). And the sign of translation continually tells, or 'tolls' the different times and spaces between cultural authority and its performative practices. The 'time' of translation consists in that *movement* of meaning, the principle and practice of a communication that, in the words of de Man, 'puts the original in motion to decanonize it, giving it the movement of fragmentation a wandering of errance, a kind of permanent exile'. (Bhabha, 1994)

Translation as a sign of fragmentation, of cultural destabilisation and negotiation is a powerful image for the late twentieth century. And as English extends its international influence, so more and more people outside the English-speaking world actively participate in translational activity. Soon native speakers of English will be disadvantaged in a world that is predominantly multilingual.

So where does this leave us? Actually, at a very good point to move forward. Both translation studies and cultural studies have come of age. Both interdisciplines have entered a new internationalist phase, and have been moving for some time away from their more overtly parochial and Eurocentric beginnings, towards a more sophisticated investigation of the relationship between the local and the global. Both are now vast wide-ranging fields, within which there is no consensus, but neither are there radical disagreements that threaten fragmentation or destruction from within. There are now clearly several areas that would lend themselves fruitfully to greater cooperation between practitioners of both interdisciplines.

- There needs to be more investigation of the acculturation process that takes place between cultures and the way in which different cultures construct their image of writers and texts.
- There needs to be more comparative study of the ways in which texts become cultural capital across cultural boundaries.
- There needs to be greater investigation of what Venuti has called 'the ethnocentric violence of translation' and much more research into the politics of translating.
- There needs to be a pooling of resources to extend research into intercultural training and the implications of such training in today's world.

It is not accidental that the genre of travel literature is providing such a rich field for exploration by both translation studies and cultural studies practitioners, for this is the genre in which individual strategies employed by writers deliberately to construct images of other cultures for consumption by readers can be most clearly seen.

In pointing out that none of us are able to comprehend fully the entirety of the complex network of signs that constitutes a culture, Raymond Williams effectively freed us from the old myth of the definitive version of anything. His thesis also offers a way forward that invites a collaborative approach, for if the totality is denied the individual, then a combination of individuals with different areas of expertise and different interests must surely be advantageous. Both cultural studies and translation studies have tended to move in the direction of the collaborative approach, with the establishment of research teams and groups, and with more international networks and increased communication. What we can see from both cultural studies and translation studies today is that the moment of the isolated academic sitting in an ivory tower is over, and indeed in these multifaceted interdisciplines, isolation is counterproductive. Translation is, after all, dialogic in its very nature, involving as it does more than one voice. The study of translation, like the study of culture, needs a plurality of voices. And, similarly, the study of culture always involves an examination of the processes of encoding and decoding that comprise translation.

References

Alvarez, Roman and Vidal, Africa (eds) (1996) *Translation, Power, Subversion.* Clevedon: Multilingual Matters.
Bassnett, Susan (1997) *Studying British Cultures: An Introduction.* London: Routledge.
Bassnett, Susan and Lefevere, André (eds) (1990) *Translation, History and Culture.* London: Pinter. (Reprinted, Cassell: 1995).
Bhabha, Homi (1994) *The Location of Culture.* London and New York: Routledge.
Bourdieu, Pierre and Passeron, J.C. (1977) *Reproduction in Education, Society and Culture.* Transl. R. Nice. London/Beverley Hills: Sage.
Dollimore, Jonathan and Sinfield, Alan (eds) (1985) *Political Shakespeare. Essays in Cultural Materialism.* Manchester: Manchester University Press.
Dronke, Peter (1968) *The Medieval Lyric.* London: Hutchinson.
Easthope, Anthony (1991) *Literary into Cultural Studies.* London: Routledge.
Easthope, Anthony (1997) But what *is* Cultural Studies? In Susan Bassnett (ed.) *Studying British Cultures: An Introduction* (pp. 3–18). London: Routledge.
Even-Zohar, Itamar (1978a) The position of translated literature within the literary polysystem. In James Holmes, Jose Lambert and Raymond van den Broek (eds) *Literature and Translation* (pp. 117–127). Leuven: ACCO.
Even-Zohar, Itamar (1978b) *Papers in Historical Poetics.* In *Papers on Poetics and Semiotics Series*, no. 8. Tel Aviv: Tel Aviv University Publishing Projects.
Even-Zohar, Itamar (1990) Polysystems studies. *Poetics Today* 11 (1), Spring.
Even-Zohar, Itamar and Toury, Gideon (eds) (1981) *Translation Theory and Intercultural Relations.* Special Issue of *Poetics Today* 2 (4), Summer/Autumn.
Gentzler, Edwin (1993) *Contemporary Translation Theories.* London and New York: Routledge.
Hall, Stuart (1991) The local and the global: Globalization and ethnicity. In Anthony D. King (ed.) *Culture, Globalization and the World-System* (pp. 19–41). London: Macmillan.
Hoggart, Richard (1957) *The Uses of Literacy.* Harmondsworth: Penguin.
Holmes, James (1988) *Translated! Papers on Literary Translation and Translation Studies.* Amsterdam: Rodopi.
Johnson, Randall (1987) Tupy or not Tupy: Cannibalism and nationalism in contemporary Brazilian literature. In John King (ed.) *Modern Latin American Fiction: A Survey* (pp. 41–59). London: Faber and Faber.
Johnson, Richard (1986) The story so far: and further transformations. In David Punter (ed.) *Introduction to Contemporary Cultural Studies* (pp. 277–314). London: Longman.
Leavis, F.R. (1930) *Mass Civilisation and Minority Culture.* (Minority Pamphlets No. 1). Cambridge: Gordon Fraser.
Lefevere, André (1978) Translation studies: The goal of the discipline. In James Holmes, Jose Lambert and Raymond van den Broek (eds) *Literature and Translation* (pp. 234–235). Leuven: ACCO.
Lefevere, André (1992) *Translation, Rewriting and the Manipulation of Literary Fame.* London and New York: Routledge.
Nida, Eugene (1954) *Customs and Cultures.* New York: Harper and Row.

Niranjana, Tejaswini (1992) *Siting Translation: History, Poststructuralism and the Colonial Context*. Berkeley, Los Angeles: University of California Press.

Simon, Sherry (1996a) Translation and interlingual creation in the contact zone. Paper for Translation as Cultural Transmission Seminar, Concordia University, Montreal.

Simon, Sherry (1996b) *Gender Translation. Cultural Identity and the Politics of Transmission*. London and New York: Routledge.

Soyinka, Wole (1976) *Myth, Literature and the African World*. Cambridge: Cambridge University Press.

Straw, Will (1993) Shifting boundaries, lines of descent. In Vanda Blundell, John Shepherd and Ian Taylor (eds) *Relocating Cultural Studies* (pp. 86–105). London and New York: Routledge.

Thompson, E.P. (1963) *The Making of the English Working Class*. London: Gollancz.

Venuti, Lawrence (1995) *The Translator's Invisibility*. London and New York: Routledge.

Williams, Raymond (1957) *Culture and Society 1780–1950*. Harmondsworth: Penguin.

Index